Paul Williams and Clive Anderson

Day One

Series Editor: Brian H Edwards

Day One

Israel
Land of promise, faith and beauty

The promised land

Israel forms a bridge between the three great continents of Africa, Asia and Europe and some of the most powerful and revolving armies have marched through this land on their way to victory or defeat.

The name 'Israel' originated in Genesis 32:28 where God gives a new name to Jacob. It is a country that borders Lebanon in the north, Syria and Jordan in the east, and Egypt on the southwest. The Israeli coastal plain on the shores of the Mediterranean is home to seventy percent of the nation's population. The Jordan River runs from Mount Hermon through the Hula Valley and the Sea of Galilee to the Dead Sea, the lowest point on the surface of the Earth.

Israel is a very small country; the distance from 'Dan to Beersheba' is a mere 150 miles. Nevertheless it remains a land of great contrasts. Within its narrow borders you will find mountains and valleys, deserts and fertile fields, plateaus and lowlands, salt water and fresh

springs. One can sunbathe in the subtropical heat of fashionable Eilat or ski on the slopes of towering Mount Hermon—and all during the same season.

For the visitor today, none of the sights and sounds of 21st century Israel can take away the fact that this is a very ancient land. Three and half thousand years ago God promised that Israel was 'a land for which the lord your God cares; the eyes of the LORD your God are always on it, from the beginning of the year to the very end of the year' (Deuteronomy 11:12). For many, it is indeed the 'Promised' land.

Facing page: Fishing is still a thriving business on the Sea of Galilee

---

The Kibbutz

'Kibbutz Ginosar' is a typical Israeli kibbutz. The kibbutz movement started in 1909, when Degania Kibbutz pioneers first arrived in Israel from Eastern Europe. The aim of these communities was to settle land, and the Hebrew word 'kibbutz' literally means 'communal settlers'.

The original principle of the kibbutz was based on the idea of joint ownership. Property is commonly owned by the members. Almost everything in the village is communal—the classroom, the dining hall, the class and the sports centre. Married couples have their own small apartment but the children are cared for in a nursery. The

kibbutz system really thrived at the time when independent farming was not practical. Today there are 270 kibbutzim in Israel, which accounts for 2% of the population. Tourists can sample the kibbutz way of life by staying at hotels attached to the kibbutz. The choice of accommodation will vary from budget to luxurious.

110km (71mi) south at 393m (1290ft) below sea-level. Not surprisingly, the name 'Jordan' actually means 'going down' or 'descender'. In Old Testament

times the rich vegetation along side the Jordan provided a safe haven for lions. John the Baptist carried out his ministry around the Jordan and it was in this river

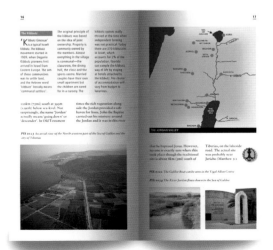

THE JORDAN VALLEY

PIX 0013 An aerial view of the North western part of the Sea of Galilee and the city of Tiberias.

that he baptised Jesus. However, no-one is exactly sure where this took place though the traditional site is about 8km (5mi) south of

Tiberias, on the lakeside road. The actual site was probably near Jericho (Matthew 3:1

PIX 0112 The Galilee Boat can be seen in the Yigal Allon Centre

PIX 0024 The River Jordan flows down to the Sea of Galilee

CONTENTS

© Day One Publications 2008 First printed 2008

A CIP record is held at The British Library   ISBN 978-1-84625-136-8

Published by Day One Publications Ryelands Road, Leominster, HR6 8NZ

✆ 01568 613 740 FAX 01568 611 473 email: sales@dayone.co.uk www.dayone.co.uk All rights reserved

Design: studiohope limited, www.studiohope.co.uk Printed by Polskabook, Poland

The promised land

Israel forms a bridge between the three great continents of Africa, Asia and Europe and some of the most powerful and terrifying armies have marched through this land on their way to victory or defeat.

The name 'Israel' originated in Genesis 32:28 where God gave a new name to Jacob. It is a country that borders Lebanon in the north, Syria and Jordan in the east, and Egypt on the southwest The Israeli coastal plain on the shores of the Mediterranean is home to seventy percent of the nation's population. The Jordan River runs from Mount Hermon through the Hula Valley and the Sea of Galilee to the Dead Sea, the lowest point on the surface of the Earth.

Israel is a very small country; the distance from 'Dan to Beersheba' is a mere 150 miles. Nevertheless it remains a land of great contrasts. Within its narrow borders you will find mountains and valleys, deserts and fertile fields, plateaux and lowlands, salt water and fresh springs. One can sunbathe in the subtropical heat of fashionable Eilat or ski on the slopes of towering Mount Hermon—and all during the same season.

For the visitor today, none of the sights and sounds of 21st century Israel can take away the fact that this is a very ancient land. Three and half thousand years ago God promised that Israel was 'a land for which the LORD your God cares; the eyes of the LORD your God are always on it, from the beginning of the year to the very end of the year' (Deuteronomy 11:12). For many, it is indeed the 'Promised' land.

Facing page: Fishing is still a thriving business on the Sea of Galilee

1 Walking on water

Israel is the ultimate visual aid for those who want to appreciate more clearly the central message of the Bible. It is the land where Jesus Christ lived, died and rose again. For this reason some people have called the land of Israel 'The Fifth Gospel'

Jesus of Nazareth carried out much of his ministry around the Sea of Galilee. In fact, some of the towns which were most prominent during his earthly life are right here on the shores of 'The Lake'. No visit to Israel is complete without sailing on the Sea of Galilee. Most boats set out from Tiberias, and from Capernaum the journey usually takes about 45 minutes. Another destination could be the Ein Gev Kibbutz. The Golan Heights are on the eastern side of the Sea, and most boats will stop for a few minutes away from the shore so that you can appreciate the quietness of the water and recall Jesus saying to Simon Peter, 'Launch out into the deep and let down your nets for a catch' (Luke 5:4). It will also put other significant events into perspective, such as the calling of Simon Peter and Andrew (Matthew 4:18), and Jesus walking on the water (Matthew 14:25).

The main city beside the Lake is Tiberias, which was built in the years AD 17 to 22 by Herod Antipas (son of Herod the Great) in honour of the Roman Emperor Tiberius. Following the destruction of Jerusalem in AD 70, Tiberias became the most

Facing page: The Horns of Hattin can be clearly seen from the Sea of Galilee

Above: *Sailing on Blue Galilee is one of the highlights of visiting Israel*

important centre of Judaism for seven hundred years. From the 3rd century it was the seat of the Jewish Council (Sanhedrin). The Jewish Mishna (AD 200) and the Talmud (AD 400) were edited here. In this city is the tomb of Rabbi Moses Ben Maimon, or Maimonides, the greatest Jewish theologian of the Middle Ages. He was a humanist, astronomer, scientist and philosopher. He died in AD 1204. Other famous Jewish scholars such as Rabbi Akiva are also buried here.

The Sea of Galilee

There are only two main areas of water within Israel: the Sea of Galilee and the Dead Sea. No fish can survive in the Dead Sea, whilst the Sea of Galilee contains a plentiful supply of catfish, mullet, sardine, carp and others. The most popular fish for tourists is St Peter's fish (Tilapia)—a 'must' to sample for any visitor to the region.

The Sea of Galilee is called by different names in the Bible. In the Old Testament it is 'Chinnereth' or 'Kinnereth' (Numbers 34:11; Joshua 12:3). In the New Testament it is referred to as 'the Sea of Tiberias' (John 6:1) and sometimes 'Gennesaret' (Luke 5:1). The Modern Hebrew spelling is 'Kinneret', taken from 'Kinnor' which means 'lute' or 'harp' because the sea is shaped rather like a harp.

The Sea of Galilee stretches 22km (15 mi) from north to south and roughly 13km (8mi) across, filling part of the valley between the hills of Galilee and the Golan Heights. With high mountains on each side and the heat above the water drawing in the cool air from the north, the wind sometimes rushes down across the surface of the water, turning the calm lake into a raging sea. Perhaps this was the situation in Mark 6:45–52 when a sudden violent storm was stilled by Jesus' command. Although the surface of the lake is at 207m (680ft) below sea level, the water is fresh.

With a population of nearly forty thousand people, Tiberias is the busiest city by the Sea of Galilee today. Nevertheless, the only mention of Tiberias in the Bible is found in John 6:23, reminding us that many came across the sea from this city to Capernaum, near the place where Jesus fed the five thousand. Sick and infirm people have been coming to the hot springs at the

Above: *First-time visitors to Israel are often surprised to see beautiful flowers growing so abundantly*

Above: *On the shore at Tiberias looking across to the Golan Heights*

southern edge of the city for more than two thousand years. The springs are highly concentrated with minerals and salts, and it is claimed that the waters have been particularly helpful to those suffering with rheumatism and arthritis. Perhaps this explains the high population in this area of Galilee.

'Galilee of the Gentiles'

Galilee is only mentioned six times in the Old Testament. But it is significant for the Christian as the boyhood home of Jesus. He spent his early years in the lower hills, and made a number of preaching tours throughout Galilee during his ministry (Matthew 4:23–25; 9:35–10:15; 11:1–6). All but one of his disciples were Galileans. It was here that Jesus foretold his death and resurrection, and set his face towards the Cross (Matthew 19:1). He met the disciples here after his resurrection, (John 21:1–14). In this region Jesus also

gave them the Great Commission (Matthew 28:16–20).

In Bible times, Galilee was separated from Judea by Samaria and it was totally surrounded by hostile, non-Jewish peoples. It should not surprise us to learn that the Jewish leaders in Jerusalem scorned the 'religious impurity' of the Galileans. The Old Testament prophet Isaiah refers to 'Galilee of the Gentiles' (Isaiah 9:1), owing to its distance from Jerusalem which was the religious heart of Israel.

The Galileans themselves were a rough, rugged people, who resisted Roman rule even more stubbornly than the Judeans. They were regarded as uneducated, uncultured and unruly. This partly explains the question posed by Nathaniel: 'Can anything good come out of Nazareth?' (John 1:46).

The Horns of Hattin

The Horns of Hattin is a seven-mile ridge that looks rather

Above: *Beneath a modern church lies the possible site of Peter's home*

like the horns of an animal, and is visible to the north-west of Tiberias. At the time of the Crusades the land of Israel had been overtaken by Muslims. The Crusaders were trying to recapture the land, and the two opposing forces came to a final conflict here at the Horns of Hattin on 4 July 1187. The Muslims won a crucial victory under the leadership of Saladin. This decisive battle helped bring an end to the period of the Crusades, although the Crusaders remained in the land until the late 13th century (See Nimrod's Castle page 30).

To the north-east of Capernaum lies the 'Anti-Lebanon' mountain range. The snow-capped peak is Mount Hermon, standing more than 2750m (9000ft) high and 30km (20mi) across. It is the most stunning mountain in the Middle East. In the Old Testament, Mount Hermon formed the northern boundary of the territory of Israel (Deuteronomy 4:47–48) and is probably the location of Jesus' transfiguration, (Matthew 17:1–13).

Bethsaida

Clockwise round the sea from Capernaum the traveller crosses the River Jordan, and 3km (2mi) further on are the ruins of Tel Beit Zaida. This site is believed to be the biblical Bethsaida, the birthplace of Peter, Andrew, James, John and Philip (John 1:44). Jesus led a blind man out of this city and healed him (Mark 8:22–26).

Capernaum

Capernaum is just over 3km (2mi) west from where the River Jordan feeds into the Sea of Galilee. Here it is possible to appreciate a great prophecy in Isaiah 9:1–2 'The people who walked in darkness have seen a great light …', and its fulfilment in Matthew 4:12–17.

Following the arrest of John the Baptist by Herod Antipas, Jesus travelled to Capernaum 'by the sea' to begin his ministry. This is the place that was referred to as the 'home of Jesus' (Mark 2:1). No other place, not even Jerusalem, was described in this way. It was here that Jesus performed many of his miracles: the healing of numerous people (Mark 1:32–34), the man let down through the roof (Mark 2:1–12), the servant of a centurion (Luke 7:1–10), the healing of the woman who touched the hem of his clothes, and the raising of Jairus's daughter (Mark 5:21–43)).

Today, the main focus of attention here is the ancient synagogue which is found in the north-east corner of Capernaum. It is a 4th or 5th century building with signs of Roman architecture. Even though this structure did not exist during Jesus' ministry, archaeologists have found parts of an earlier building of black basalt stone; it is possible that these are the remains of the synagogue the centurion gave to the town (Luke 7:4–5). If so, what can be seen today was built, following the usual practice, on the site of the 1st century synagogue where Jesus taught and preached (Mark 1:21; Luke 4:31–33, and John 6:59).

Among the ruins around the ancient synagogue in Capernaum, stands a monument with the inscription 'Via Maris,' or 'the way of the sea'. Capernaum was located directly on the road that was used by Gentiles as a through route travelling between Europe, Asia and Africa. There was no better place for Jesus to begin his ministry or to symbolise the worldwide outreach of the gospel. See the Box: The Via Maris on page 51.

Opposite the synagogue there is a Roman Catholic Church building that looks strangely out of place. It has been built over the site of an ancient house, believed to be the site of Peter's home in Capernaum. If so, it would have been here that Jesus healed Peter's mother-in-law (Luke 4:38–39). It is well-worth noting some other items of interest nearby. There are various pieces of black basalt stone on display, finely carved with significant images such as a candelabra and the Star of David. Towards the waterside there is a carefully carved image of the Ark of the Covenant mounted on wheels.

Above: *Capernaum was the hometown of Simon Peter*

Left: The Via Maris milestone in Capernum marked the ancient highway

Right: In the ruined synagogue at Chorazin, the Seat of Moses is a basalt armchair which was kept for the important members of the community

Far right: Through the arches at the Chapel of the Beatitudes

Chorazin

Chorazin (Korazin, Luke 10:13–15), lies just north-east of Capernaum. Taking the road west from Capernaum, after 3km (2mi) a road turns sharply right uphill away from the sea. Within 5km (3mi) is Chorazin. Excavations carried out since 1962 have revealed a large mikveh (ritual bath) and an ancient synagogue.

The ruins remain largely overgrown as a silent testimony to the truth of Christ's warning of God's judgement upon the cities of Bethsaida, Capernaum and Chorazin. Christ cursed them for their unbelief and failure to repent (Matthew 11:21). All three cities are still in ruins today, while Tiberias thrives.

Above: A 4th century limestone synagogue at Capernaum contrasts with the black basalt foundations which are almost certainly part of a synagogue from the time of Jesus

The Mount of Beatitudes

Following the road around the Sea of Galilee brings the traveller to the site traditionally regarded as the place where Jesus preached the Sermon on the Mount. In the heat of Galilee it provides a welcome shade under the trees. A grove of palm trees leads to the Chapel of the Beatitudes, built with vividly contrasting black basalt and white edging. There are breathtaking sweeping views across the Sea of Galilee from the walkway around the Chapel. It is worthwhile spending time here to sit and read again the Sermon on the Mount (Matthew chapters 5–7). One of the many natural bays that can be seen from here helps to bring to life Jesus teaching in a boat (Matthew 13:2).

Tabgha

For those visitors who are able, there is a fairly short, yet pleasant walk down from the Chapel of the Beatitudes across the field to Tabgha (or 'Heptapegon'), the Church of the Multiplication.

Traditionally this is the site where Jesus fed the five thousand, although the Bible places it near Bethsaida just east from the River Jordan (Luke 9:10). In the church are mosaics, discovered in 1932, of a church dating back to the 4th century AD. The mosaic floor shows some of the flowers and wildlife that probably would have been abundant during Christ's ministry. Here is a dove on a lotus flower, a goose with an oleander bush, a bird attacking a snake, and there are swans, cranes, wild geese and storks. The wall mosaic at the front of the church shows a basket of loaves with an upright fish on either side. This recalls that great miracle of Christ feeding the multitude (Matthew 14:13–21).

Mensa Christi

On the sea shore next to the Church of The Multiplication, is the Church of St Peter's Primacy, or Mensa Christi ('Table of Christ'). It was built in 1943 on the ruins of an earlier church,

Above left: Looking down across the bay from The Chapel of The Beatitudes

Above right: Excavations at Tabgha revealed a 4th century AD floor mosaic of the loaves and the fishes

which itself was built on a huge rock which has been called 'The Table of Christ' It is believed that this is where Jesus prepared a breakfast of fish and bread for his disciples following his resurrection (John 21:9–14). It was also here that Jesus re-commissioned Peter with the words, 'Feed my sheep' (John 21:15–17).

Magdala

Just before reaching Magdala is Ginossar, one of the many kibbutzim in Israel. It is also well-known since the discovery of the 'Galilee Boat'. (See the

Boxes: The Galilee Boat and The Kibbutz pages 15–16). Just 5km (3mi) north of Tiberias there are some excavations between the main road and the sea. The fenced area is owned by the Franciscans and this is not open to the public. According to tradition this town was the birthplace of Mary Magdalene. During Christ's ministry, Magdala was an important fishing port. The Jewish historian Josephus, writing towards the end of the 1st century, refers to this town. He records that there were forty thousand people living here and 230 fishing boats in use.

Kursi

Kursi is located on the east side of the Sea of Galilee, 6km (4mi) north of Ein Gev kibbutz at the junction road leading out to the Golan Heights. In 1970, the remains of an ancient site were discovered during road construction here. Archaeologists found that this was the largest Byzantine monastery in Israel. From the extensive mosaics unearthed, it is believed that this

The Galilee Boat (or 'Jesus Boat')

During 1985 and 1986 the water level in the Sea of Galilee was greatly reduced due to a severe drought. Two brothers, Moshe and Yuval Lufan, who had an interest in archaeology, took this rare opportunity to search the newly exposed lake bed. In January 1986 they discovered some ancient bronze coins, and soon after, the oval shape of a boat covered by the mud. Mendel Nun, the local expert in Galilee, quickly recognised the significance of this discovery and informed the Israeli Department of Antiquities.

Archaeologists found that the wooden planks of the hull were joined in a way that dated back to ancient times. The boat was carefully removed from the mud and placed in a tank containing a synthetic wax to preserve the 'Galilee Boat'. Measuring 8m (26ft) long, 2·3m (7·5ft) wide and 1·4m (4·5ft) high, it looks very similar to a boat pictured in a 1st century AD mosaic at Capernaum. Carbon dating places this fishing vessel at somewhere between 120 BC and 40 AD, which means that the Galilee Boat may be very similar to the kind used by the first disciples Peter, Andrew, James and John. It is worthwhile visiting the Yigal Allon Museum to see this fascinating archaeological discovery.

marked the place where Jesus cast out demons from the Gadarene demoniac, driving a herd of pigs into the sea (Luke 8:26–39). Historically, this region of the Lake has long been considered by Jews to be an evil place. It is referred to as 'Kurshi' in the Talmud (early Jewish teachings) and as being a centre of idol worship. Kursi is open to the public for those who wish to visit.

Susita

5km (3mi) south from Kursi on the east side of the sea is Susita, better known as the ruins of the ancient city Hippos. Directly across from Tiberias, it is situated at 305m (1000ft) above the level of the Lake. Hippos was the major city of the Decapolis region and it dates from 332 BC. It is most likely the place that Jesus referred to when he said to his disciples: 'You are the light of the world. A city that is set on a hill cannot be hidden' (Matthew 5:14).

The River Jordan

The River Jordan begins at the foot of Mount Hermon, where several springs join together. The river then flows down from

Above: *The Church of St Peter's Primacy recalls the restoration of Peter by the shore of Galilee*

Opposite: *The Chapel of The Beatitudes overlooks Galilee*

The Kibbutz

'Kibbutz Ginossar' is a typical Israeli kibbutz. The kibbutz movement started in 1909, when Degania Kibbutz pioneers first arrived in Israel from Eastern Europe. The aim of these communities was to settle land, and the Hebrew word 'kibbutz' literally means 'communal settlers'.

The original principle of the kibbutz was based on the idea of joint ownership. Property is commonly owned by the members. Almost everything in the village is communal—the classroom, the dining hall, the clinic and the sports centre. Married couples have their own small apartment but the children are cared for in a nursery. The kibbutz system really thrived at the time when independent farming was not practical. Today there are 270 kibbutzim in Israel, which accounts for 2% of the population. Tourists can sample the kibbutz way of life by staying at hotels attached to the kibbutz. The choice of accommodation will vary from budget to luxurious.

the northern part of a great rift valley, which runs down through the Gulf of Aqaba to the great Lakes of East Africa. The head-waters begin at 70m (230ft) above sea level and enter the Dead Sea 120km (75mi) south at 393m (1290ft) below sea-level. Not surprisingly, the name 'Jordan' actually means 'going down' or 'descender'. In Old Testament times the rich vegetation alongside the Jordan provided a safe haven for lions. John the Baptist carried out his ministry around the Jordan and it was in this river that he baptised Jesus. However, no-one is exactly sure where this took place though the traditional site is about 8km (5mi) south of Tiberias, on the lakeside road. The actual site was probably near Jericho (Matthew 3:1 to 4:12).

Below right: The Galilee Boat can be seen in the Yigal Allon Centre
Below left: The River Jordan flows down to the Sea of Galilee

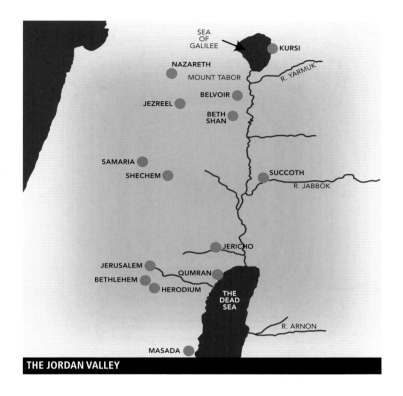

SEA
OF
GALILEE

KURSI

NAZARETH

MOUNT TABOR

R. YARMUK

BELVOIR

JEZREEL

BETH
SHAN

SAMARIA

SHECHEM

SUCCOTH

R. JABBOK

JERICHO

JERUSALEM

QUMRAN

BETHLEHEM

HERODIUM

THE
DEAD
SEA

R. ARNON

MASADA

THE JORDAN VALLEY

Below: An aerial view of the north western part of the Sea of Galilee and the city of Tiberias

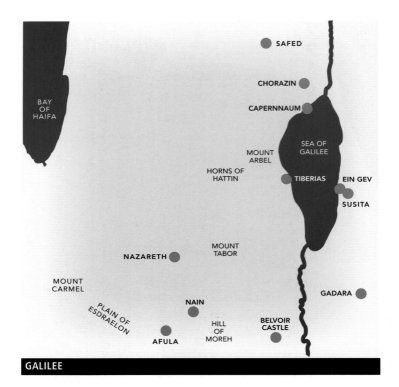

SAFED

CHORAZIN

CAPERNNAUM

BAY
OF
HAIFA

SEA OF
GALILEE

MOUNT
ARBEL

HORNS OF
HATTIN

TIBERIAS

EIN GEV

SUSITA

MOUNT
TABOR

NAZARETH

MOUNT
CARMEL

PLAIN OF
ESDRAELON

NAIN

GADARA

HILL
OF
MOREH

BELVOIR
CASTLE

AFULA

GALILEE

Above: *Sunset over Galilee*

Unless otherwise noted most places in this travel section will be found on the websites: http://www.science.co.il/nature.asp OR www.sacred-destinations.com

Ein Gev

At Ein Gev Kibbutz there is an excellent fish restaurant which serves St Peter's fish. The chef will fillet the fish for any who require it to be done.

Capernaum

Driving down to the shores of Kinneret, and then turning eastward, two miles along the coast reach the ruins of Capernaum (Kfar Nahum in Hebrew; the village of Nahum). Walking from the parking area pass the Franciscan monastery on the right, while in the adjacent courtyard lie the ruins of the synagogue and the possible home of the Apostle Peter.

Kursi

☏ (04) 6731983
Directions: Kursi junction is on Route

Above: Yardenit is the site where Christians are baptised in the River Jordan

92 (east of the Sea of Galilee), 5km (3mi) north of Ein Gev. Turn east at the junction and follow the sign to Kursi National Park, which is about 50m (160ft) past the junction.

Open: April–September: 0800–17:00; October–March: 0800–16:00

Chorazin

📞 (04) 6934982
Directions: Chorazin National Park is on Route 90 between Chorazin junction and Almagor,

CAPHARNAUM THE TOWN OF JESUS

Above: Capernaum, or Kfar Nahum, means village of Nahum

10 minutes east of Amiad junction.
Open: April–September: 0800–17:00; October–March: 0800–1600

Yardenit—the traditional site for baptisms

At the southernmost tip of the Lake, you reach the point where the river Jordan once again

starts its long flow south toward the Dead Sea. Take the left turn immediately after crossing the bridge over the River Jordan, and turn toward Kvuzat Kinneret until you see the large parking area on your left: you have arrived at the Yardenit, a baptismal site with safe access to the river and full facilities for visitors.

Above: Corazim/Korazim is a National Park

② Look to the hills

The melt water from Mount Hermon joins the head waters of the Jordan, rushing into a powerful cascade at Banias; if ever there was a place to refute the idea that the whole of Israel is a desert, it is northern Galilee. In such a lush and bountiful location, Peter made his great confession

The former city of Hazor lies just to the north of the Sea of Galilee. In Joshua's day, it was the stronghold of the Canaanites, and the chief northern city (Joshua 11:10). Therefore, it was of strategic importance. Originally captured by Joshua, it was later rebuilt by Solomon as one of his chariot towns (1 Kings 9:15). Subsequently, it was one of the first cities to be destroyed by the Assyrian King, Tiglath-Pileser III, in 732 BC (2 Kings 15:29).

When Professor Yigael Yadin led the excavations here in 1968–69, he discovered a water shaft that King Ahab's men had constructed by digging down 38m (125ft) to the water source. The excavations are extensive, covering two distinct sections: the upper city (the acropolis) and lower city (the fortified enclosure) lying to the north. At the time of David and Solomon, Hazor was roughly ten times bigger than Jerusalem. Today the ruins form one of Israel's national parks.

The drive north continues through the Hula Valley, Israel's lake country. A former swamp, it was drained in the 1950s to provide more arable land and to eradicate malaria. Since then, ecologists have realised that this is a stopover for migrating birds between Europe, Asia and Africa. As a result, the area has been set aside as a nature reserve. The Hula Nature Reserve consists of 360 hectares (800 acres) of ponds and channels, with turtles, water buffalo, and more than 200 species of birds which flock here in their tens of thousands, including storks, pelicans and cranes.

Mount Hermon

Travelling north through the Hula Valley, Mount Hermon soon becomes visible. It is the southernmost ridge of the Anti-Lebanon Mountains—not one single mountain but a range of peaks ('the heights of Hermon' of Psalm 42) the highest of which rises to 2750m (9000ft). The peaks are topped with snow most of the time and some snow remains even through the summer.

No trees grow above the snow line, but the lower slopes are covered with pine, oak, and

Facing page: The copious waters flow from Mount Hermon into Dan National Park

Above: *Mount Hermon is a high mountain range in Israel*

poplar, along with vineyards. Wolves, leopards, and bears live in the forests. The word Hermon means 'a consecrated place, a sanctuary'. Today the Arabs call the height Jebel esh-Sheikh, 'the mountain of the chief' or Jabel eth-Thalj, 'mountain of snow'. Two of the four sources of the Jordan River begin at the foot of Mount Hermon and then flow south. The Leddan at Tell el-Qad (Dan) and the Banias at Banias (Caesarea Philippi) originate in underground springs.

Mount Hermon is not specifically named in the New Testament. However, some scholars believe that one of its peaks was the 'high mountain' on which the favoured disciples saw Jesus transfigured (Matthew 17:1–8). Tradition locates this event on Mount Tabor, roughly 70km (45mi) from Caesarea Philippi, although the Gospels make no mention of such a long journey to the Mount of Transfiguration. Caesarea

Philippi lies at the south-western end of Mount Hermon, making this range the most likely place for the transfiguration. Mount Hermon is mentioned occasionally in the Old Testament (see Deuteronomy 3:8–9; Psalm 89:12; 133:3; Song of Solomon 4:8). The territory came under the control of Herod the Great in 20 BC and was passed on to his son Philip the Tetrarch at his death in 4 BC; Philip ruled the area until AD 33. Titus and Vespasian camped their armies near Caesarea Philippi during the Jewish revolt of AD 66–70. In more recent times, Mount Hermon has been developed into a skiing centre.

Located on the south-western slopes of Mount Hermon, some 6km (4mi) apart, are Dan and Caesarea Philippi. The expression 'from Dan to Beersheba' occurs a number of times in the Bible (for example in Judges 20:1 and I Samuel 3:20), representing the northernmost and southernmost

Above: Peter made his confession at Caesarea Philippi

areas of the land of Israel. So, when Jesus visited Caesarea Philippi he was at the very northernmost tip of the land. The word Dan means 'judge' and the city is located at Tell el-Qadi which means 'mound of the judge'.

Dan

Dan is best remembered in biblical history with the account of Jeroboam I (931–910 BC), the first king of the northern kingdom of Israel. At one time, Dan was the most northerly town in Israel. Following the death of Solomon, the kingdom divided under Rehoboam in the south (two tribes) and Jeroboam in the north (ten tribes). Jeroboam led the people into idolatrous worship. 1 Kings 12:26–28 records that in order to try and dissuade them from attending the temple services in Jerusalem he ordered two golden calves to be cast, and then proclaimed them to be Israel's gods. One was set up in Bethel and the other at Dan.

In 1966 a team began to excavate Tel Dan (the word 'tel' is an Arabic word for a ruin

Below: The excavated entrance of Dan

Dan National Park

Until the 1967 Six Day War, the Dan River was the only source of the River Jordan in Israeli hands. However, with water being so scarce, it was necessary to use water from the Dan River to meet the needs of the population. This almost spelt the end for the reserve. But conservationists fought their case and in 1969 Dan National Park was established.

A trail walk through Dan National Park is well worth it. Bubbling brooks feed into a fast-running river and tall trees stretch up to the sky, providing shade so that the ground is always cool even at noon on a hot summer's day. It makes a refreshing change for the tourist. Of the sources of the River Jordan, the Dan is the largest and most important. The springs are fed by the snow and rain that fall on Mt. Hermon, providing up to 1·5 billion cubic metres (52 billion gallons) of water each year. The water seeps into the mountain, dividing into hundreds of springs by the time it reaches the foot of Hermon. Although Dan National Park only covers around 55 hectares (120 acres), its location and unique environment makes it rich in flora and fauna.

mound). The impressive findings included sections of imposing walls and gates, as well as a ritual site that dates to the time of dramatic events recounted in the Bible. The earliest findings from a settlement on Tel Dan date back to the beginning of the 5th century BC. Tel Dan is identified with the city of Laish, captured by the tribe of Dan. They found it difficult to deal with the Philistines, and

Below: *The Gates of the ancient city of Dan*

Above: *This altar in Dan National Park was originally built by Jeroboam I in the late 10th century BC and rebuilt by Jeroboam II in the 8th century BC*

therefore decided to move north (Judges 18:27–29).

One of the fascinating finds from Tel Dan is a piece of black basalt stone (The Tel Dan Stele) which dates from the 9th or 8th centuries BC. Carved onto it is an inscription of Hazael, King of Damascus (he is referred to in 2 Kings 8:8), boasting of his victory over the king of Israel and the king of the House of David. This is the first time that the words 'house of David' were discovered outside of the Bible. Unfortunately, archaeologists

Below: *A view into Lebanon from Tel Dan lookout post*

have yet to find the inscription in its entirety. Dan continued to be inhabited until the Roman period. It was then abandoned, and the centre of settlement moved to Banias.

Banias—Caesarea Philippi

A few minutes drive from Dan is the majestic power of the Banias waterfall. Just over 1·5km (1mi) to the east is Banias proper—the Arabic rendering for the Greek 'Paneas'. At one time a shrine for Baal (the god of fertility, rain and storm) was erected here, and later the Greeks worshipped Pan the god of shepherds, who was

---

The Golan Heights

'The Golan' is the name given to a dormant volcanic mountain range that rises on the eastern shore of the Sea of Galilee, running northwards along the Upper Jordan as far as the Hermon mountain range. The Heights of the Golan rise to about 4000 feet above sea level, and reach across into Syria. But in the Bible, the Golan was allotted to Israel as a portion of the inheritance of the half-tribe of Manasseh. The actual town of Golan was appointed as one of the Old Testament cities of refuge (Joshua 20:8).

Politically, the Golan remains a strategic part of the land of Israel. At the end of World War I the area of Golan was under Syrian control, in accordance with the French Mandate. When Syria was defeated by Israel in the War of Independence (1948), the Syrians strengthened their position on the Golan Heights and were thus able to keep Galilee under constant attack. However, at the start of the Six Days' War in 1967, the Israeli Army responded to Syria's heavy bombardment by driving out the Syrian forces. On the Golan Heights a war memorial commemorates the tank battle that took place in 1973 at the 'Vale of Tears'.

also responsible for sowing panic among the enemy. In the Roman world he was associated with the word *pan*, 'all.' So he became the universal god, '*the All*.' Niches devoted to this worship are still to be seen in the cliff face.

Caesar Augustus presented the district to Herod the Great who erected and dedicated a temple to the Emperor near to the spring. On Herod's death the territory passed to his youngest son Philip who established Banias as his capital, re-naming it Caesarea Philippi and thereby distinguishing it from Caesarea on the Mediterranean coast. This was the most northerly recorded place that Jesus travelled in his ministry.

Caesarea Philippi occurs in

Above: *A niche in the rocks at Caesarea Philippi reminds us of Peter's confession of Christ*

Opposite page: *The Golan Heights is called Bashan in the Bible*

Above: *Inside the large cave at Caesarea Philippi the river suddenly drops underground and in ancient times it was thought to be the entrance to Hell. For this reason it was called The Gates of Hell*

Above: *Birket Ram is a beautiful lake high in the hills*

the Bible only at the time when Jesus and the disciples moved 'into the district of Caesarea Philippi' (Matthew 16:13) or 'to the villages of Caesarea Philippi' (Mark 8:27). It was here that Jesus asked his disciples what the multitudes were saying about him. The disciples gave several answers, repeating the words they had heard as they moved through the crowds following Jesus. Some thought he was John the Baptist, some Elijah, (Elijah had challenged and defeated the prophets of Baal on Carmel) and still others thought he was Jeremiah (traditionally the prophet of doom) or one of the other prophets. Jesus put a second question to them, 'Who do you say that I am?' Peter answered, 'You are the Christ, the Son of the living God' (Matthew 16:15, 16). Jesus responded by blessing Peter and by telling the disciples that he would build his church upon

the rock-solid foundation that Jesus Christ is the Son of God. Then Jesus began to speak of his mission (Matthew 16:21). It is not clear whether he and his disciples ever entered Caesarea Philippi, but here he deliberately contrasts himself with the other belief systems of his day.

Leaving Banias the road climbs, passing through the Druze village of Massada which lies to the east of Majdal Shams (Tower of the Sun) the chief Druze town in the area. Although the Druze are Arabs, they are not Muslims. They practice a religion which began as an offshoot of Islam in Egypt in the 11th century AD, developing as a totally independent religion. Fleeing persecution, the Druze moved north and today they live mainly in Israel, Syria and Lebanon.

Above: Nimrod's Castle stands proudly overlooking the Golan

Below: The Golan Heights overlook Lebanon and Syria

Birket Ram (Height Pool)

Near the Druze village of Massada (not to be confused with Masada near the Dead Sea), and about 11km (7mi) east of Banias, is a beautiful natural pool called Birket Ram. This is a natural pool within the crater of an extinct volcano. Up to 30 feet deep, the water is a pleasant place to swim. There is a restaurant here, offering good simple food, including felafal (pitta bread stuffed with salad and balls of deep-fried ground chick peas, mildly spiced with peppers, and humus). In the spring, with the roses in full flower, this is an

Above: The Synagogue at Gamla

Below: Looking towards Mount Hermon from the Golan

idyllic stopping place for lunch, gazing across towards the slopes of Mount Hermon.

Nimrod's Castle

The ruins of this Crusader Castle are a well-preserved 13th century fortress overlooking the Hula valley on the slopes of Mount Hermon. The reason for the association with the biblical Nimrod (Genesis 10:8–10) is unclear. The castle played an important role in the twelfth and

Above: The silhouetted soldier on Mount Bental reminds visitors that this was a strategic military location during the six days war of 1967

thirteenth centuries AD, during the power struggle between the Crusaders and the Muslim Kingdom of Damascus.

Driving back down through the Golan, Mount Bental is a good stopping place. It also provides the finest of views across the Heights into Syria. It is situated on the edge of an extinct volcanic crater, and was used as an Israeli Defence Forces outpost. It had been forbidden to visitors, but at the time of writing the tunnels and trenches leading to the communications room, bunkers and kitchen, deep below the ground can be explored. Mount Bental and the other volcanic peaks now form the cease-fire line. To the right is Mount Avital, and to the left, one of the finest views in Israel of Mount Hermon. If you get tired of the view, why not step into the log-cabin coffee shop with the tongue-in-cheek name 'Coffee Anan', which means 'coffee in the clouds'.

Gamla

Gamla is a hill on the Golan, East of the Sea of Galilee. It is shaped like a camel's hump. Gamla is a very impressive natural fortress, rising from a valley and linked to a plateau by a narrow ridge of land. Beside the town wall is probably the only synagogue of Jesus' time yet found in Galilee.

Thousands of Jews from the Golan sought refuge here when the Roman General Vespasian, two years before he became emperor, besieged the site in AD 67. Despite initial success against the Romans the final battle saw several thousand Jews slaughtered, whilst a further thousand committed suicide by throwing themselves over the cliff.

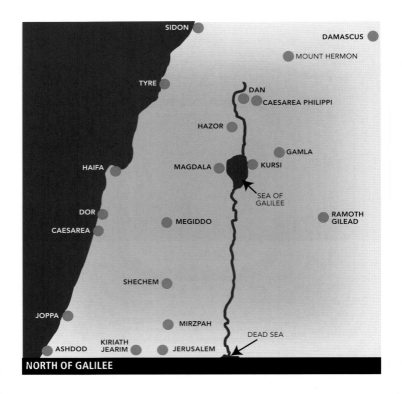

NORTH OF GALILEE

Map labels: SIDON, DAMASCUS, MOUNT HERMON, TYRE, DAN, CAESAREA PHILIPPI, HAZOR, GAMLA, HAIFA, MAGDALA, KURSI, SEA OF GALILEE, DOR, MEGIDDO, RAMOTH GILEAD, CAESAREA, SHECHEM, JOPPA, MIRZPAH, DEAD SEA, ASHDOD, KIRIATH JEARIM, JERUSALEM

Unless otherwise noted most places in this travel section will be found on the websites: http://www.science.co.il/nature.asp OR www.sacred-destinations.com

The Galilee Experience

Website: www.thegalileeexperience.com

'The Galilee Experience' is situated on the Tiberias waterfront, just ten minutes walk from the major hotels in the centre of town. It is a luxurious air-conditioned theatre, providing a superb multimedia presentation of the history of the land of Israel. During the presentation, 4,000 years of Galilee history comes to life in just 38 minutes. It gives an excellent overview of the famous men and women who made history in Galilee. There are hourly showings. 'The Galilee Experience' is owned and operated by Jewish Christians. The story of how this theatre came into existence is interesting in itself. For those buying presents the shop is highly recommended. A visit to 'The Galilee Experience' is very worthwhile. But please check the times of the showings to avoid disappointment.

Below: Getting your bearings on Mount Bental

Opposite page: A sign marks the Hermon River springs

Coffee Anan

Website: http://www.meromgolantourism.co.il/page-english.php

Coffee Anan is a coffee shop and dairy restaurant located 1164 m (3822 ft) above sea level, at the top of Mount Bental. It is owned by Kibbutz Merom Golan, offering good food and the chance to drink coffee at the highest restaurant in Israel. There are spectacular panoramic views across Lebanon, Syria and north-eastern Israel. 'Anan' means 'cloud'. There is also a gift shop with a selection of locally produced foods such as teas and jams, plus good quality craft items.

Nimrod's Castle

📞 (04) 6949277

The entrance is located on Route 989 between Qiryat Shemona and Mount Hermon, about thirty minutes east of Kiryat Shmona. The village of Nimrod is located nearby.

Open: April–September:

0800–1700; October–March: 0800–1600

Tel Dan

📞 (04) 6951579

Directions: The Tel Dan Nature Reserve is on Route 99 (Kiryat Shemona-Mas\'AD e), about 11km (7mi) east of Hamezudot junction, near Kibbutz DanOpen: April–September: 0800–1700; October–March: 0800–1600

Ceasarea Philippi Hermon National Park

📞 (04) 6902577

Directions to the spring: The spring is off Route 99 (Kiryat Shemona-Mas\'sade), east of Kibbutz Snir.

To the waterfall: From Route 99 (Kiryat Shemona-Mas\'sade) turn south about one mile east of Kibbutz Snir and follow the signs to the reserve.

Open: April–September: 0800–1700; October–March: 0800–1600

Hula Valley Nature Reserve

📞 (04) 6937069

Directions: Hula Valley Nature Reserve is on Route 90 (Rosh Pina-Kiryat Shemona). About 3km (2mi) after Yesod Hama'ale junction, turn east into the reserve.

Open: All year: 0800–1600; Friday: 0800–1500

Tel Hazor National Park

📞 (04) 6937290

Tel Hazor National Park is opposite Kibbutz Ayelet Hashar on Route 90 (Rosh Pin-Kiryat Shemona), 15 minutes north of Rosh Pina

Open: April–September: 0800–1700; October–March: 0800–1600

Gamla Nature Reserve

📞 (04) 6937290

Open: April–September: 0800–1700; October–March: 0800–1600

③ Armageddon

Throughout history, the fertile Plain of Jezreel held a strategic position commanding the trade routes between Egypt, Asia Minor and Babylon. It is not surprising that Israel's 'bread basket' has been the scene of many great battles

Megiddo

Tel Megiddo, located in the Jezreel Valley—also known as Armageddon in the Bible, (Revelation 16)—was one of the three largest settlements in the land of Israel during the reign of King Solomon. Situated by the main trade route travelling east from the coast, Megiddo's strategic position caught the attention of foreign conquerors. There are twenty five different strata of civilization here, all belonging to cultures who understood the importance of controlling the major highway. A scale model of Megiddo in the museum on the site helps explain how a tel is formed. A tel usually began as a settlement on a small hill situated near a water source, often in a strategic location not far from a major highway. When an invading army attacked the hill and destroyed the settlement the conquerors simply smoothed over the area and built their homes on the ruins. This was repeated again and again through the ages, so that the hill grew higher and higher as each conflict brought destruction and renewal. A tel is usually excavated layer by layer and not by digging a deep shaft. Peeling away each layer one at a time enables archaeologists to study each civilization in turn. The ancient city of Megiddo is located on the eastern slope of the Carmel range between Jokneam, 11km (7mi) to the northwest, and Taanach, five miles to the southeast. These three cities guarded passes through the range which provided access to the Plain

Facing page: The Biblical Village in Nazareth gives a real life impression of the time when Jesus lived here

Below: Figs grow wild in Israel

Above: A 3rd century AD church has been discovered recently in the grounds of the prison at Megiddo

of Megiddo from the coast. On the west of Megiddo, the slope of Mount Carmel protected the city from unexpected invaders from the Sharon Plain. The citizens of Megiddo enjoyed a commanding view of the Plain of Jezreel (also known as the Plain of Megiddo) below it. To the northeast they could see the ridge on which Nazareth was later built. Mount Tabor and the Hill of Moreh rise toward the eastern end of the plain. In the southwest, Mount Gilboa guarded the northern border of what was later known as Samaria. A cosmopolitan city, it lay at the crossroads of the international coastal highway and the main road connecting Shechem and the hill country of Ephraim to the Plain of Acco and Tyre and Sidon along the northern coast.

Battles in the plain of Megiddo

The plain stretching out before Megiddo has been the scene of many great battles in history; some are referred to in the Bible. The Egyptian pharaoh Tuthmosis III took Megiddo from the Canaanites in 1470 BC claiming: 'The capturing of Megiddo is the capturing of a thousand cities.' This conquest further established Egyptian presence and control of the land before the conquest under Joshua. After the conquest and settling of the land, Megiddo became one of the major cities in the area that the tribe of Manasseh was unable to overpower completely. It was Deborah from the hill country of Samaria and Barak, Israel's commander from Kedesh in the tribal area of Naphtali, whom God used to overcome the

A recent discovery has brought widespread attention to Megiddo Prison, close to Tel Megiddo. In the late 1990's the authorities decided to create more space within the prison compound. Using their own inmates as labourers, they discovered ancient remains and called in the Israel Antiquities Authority. In 2005, under the direction of archaeologist Yotam Tepper, they exposed the remains of one of the earliest Christian churches in the world, dating around 230 AD.

The most exciting find in the excavation is a well-preserved mosaic floor, unmistakably revealing it to be a Christian prayer room. One of the panels of the mosaic includes two fish, being the earliest distinct symbol for Jesus Christ—the Roman Cross did not appear until the 7th century. An inscription clearly indicates that those who worshipped here were locally based Roman soldiers, with the donor being a centurion. Another inscription proves the existence of a table in the centre of the room, paid for by a woman named Akeptous: 'The God-loving Akeptous has offered the table to God Jesus Christ as a memorial.' This is the earliest inscription ever found in Israel, perhaps the world, which mentions Jesus Christ by name. The authorities are hoping that in time, this site will become of major interest for tourists.

Canaanites of the region. Led by Jabin king of Hazor in the north, who was joined by men from cities around the Plain of Megiddo, the Canaanites gathered 'at Taanach, near the waters of Megiddo'

Below: Mount Tabor was the scene of the victory of Deborah and Barak

Above: *Looking over Nazareth today*

(Judges 5:19). In the battle that followed, Deborah and Barak led the charge from Mt Tabor against the Canaanite chariot corps which was immobilized in the 'torrent of the Kishon' (Judges 4:13–15; 5:21–25). Much later, Elijah ran 32km (20mi) this way through the Jezreel valley from Mount Carmel ahead of King Ahab's chariot (1 Kings 18:46).

Solomon fortified Megiddo, making it his stronghold (with Hazor in the upper Jordan Valley and Gezer on the Coastal Plain) to ensure his control of the international coastal highway (1 Kings 9:15–16). After Solomon's death, Shishak of Egypt destroyed Megiddo, erecting a stele on the site to mark his victory (1 Kings 14:25–28). Later still, in 874–853 BC, Ahab rebuilt the city in grand style. It was probably at Megiddo that

Pharaoh Necho killed King Josiah when he intercepted Necho to prevent him from reaching Carchemish to assist the Assyrians against the Babylonians (2 Kings 23:29–30).

Clearly then, Megiddo was one of the most strategic cities in Israel until it was finally destroyed by the Assyrians in 732 BC.

The word Armageddon derives from the Hebrew words *har* 'mount' or 'hill' and *Megiddo*. In Rev. 16:12–16, the drying up of the River Euphrates to prepare for invasion by the kings from the east (v 12), allows them to come 'to the place which in Hebrew is called Har-Magedon' (v 16). This broad plain has been the scene of over a hundred battles, including armies led by Napoleon and, in the 20th century, by General Allenby, as he delivered the region from the Turks.

Above: The Church of the Annunciation

Below: Inside the Orthodox Church of the Annunciation in Nazareth

Mount Tabor

Mount Tabor is the boundary between Issachar and Zebulun (Joshua 19:22–23). Deborah and Barak met here before defeating Sisera (Judges 4:6–17). Furthermore, it was here that Zebah and Zalmunna slew Gideon's brothers (Judges 8:18–21). The nearby settlements, Kibbutz Dovrat and the Bedouin village of Dabburiyeh, preserve the memory of those events in their names, both derived from the Hebrew, 'Deborah'.

In more recent times, this was also a scene of conflict on 16 April 1799, when French forces opposed the Ottoman army while Napoleon Bonaparte was besieging Acre and Damascus. Taken by surprise, the Ottoman force was routed.

Traditionally, Mount Tabor has been regarded as the site of the Transfiguration of Jesus and

Above left: The ancient steps down to the natural spring in Nazareth date back to the time of Jesus

Above right: The gateway to Mary's Well

a large church at the summit commemorates the account from Matthew 17. The church is built over the remains of an ancient Crusader church and fortress overlooking the Jezreel Valley. Inside are altars dedicated to Moses and Elijah, and a mosaic depicting the Transfiguration. Although this tradition goes back many centuries, some scholars believe the description of the Mount of Transfiguration as 'a high mountain' (Matthew 17:1; Mark 9:2) makes Mt. Hermon the more likely location.

Nazareth

Nazareth is Israel's largest Arab city, with about 60,000 inhabitants, half of whom are Christian and half are Muslim. Although today it is a large and bustling city, during the time of Jesus, Nazareth was a small, out-of-the-way village with probably only a few dozen families. In the Book of Joshua, twelve Galilean settlements are mentioned, without any reference to Nazareth. Therefore it is easy to understand why people reacted with disbelief when Jesus claimed to be the Messiah, from Nazareth: Nathaniel asked, 'Can anything good come out of Nazareth?'(John 1:46). It sits at 400m (1300ft) above sea level, 24km (15mi) west of the Sea of Galilee and 32km (20mi) east of the Mediterranean Sea. The city therefore has a moderate climate. From the heights around Nazareth, one can see south to the Jezreel Valley, east to Mount Tabor and north to Mount Hermon.

The Church of the Annunciation

This is Nazareth's largest and best known church. It is built

—

over the grotto where the angel Gabriel is traditionally thought to have appeared to Mary and announced that she had been chosen by God to give birth to the Saviour, Jesus Christ (Luke 1:26–28). Completed in 1966, it is probably the only church in the world built by a Jewish contractor and Muslim construction workers! Standing on the site of a former Crusader church, the building has four themes: Mary, Miracle, Modern and Multi-national. The lower floor represents the human nature of Jesus and centres around the Grotto of the Annunciation. The great bronze doors at the entrance depict scenes from the Old Testament and from the life of Jesus. Parts of a Byzantine mosaic and a Crusader wall from earlier churches have been incorporated into the area around the grotto. The upper floor focuses on Jesus as the Son of God. Its tower appears as a lighthouse or beacon from the outside, but from the inside it resembles a lily wi in the sky, opening sl walls are decorated wi ge mosaics contributed by Roman Catholic communities from all over the world, each depicting Mary, or Mary with Jesus, as they see them.

The Church of St Gabriel (Mary's Well)

This site may not be the most popular for tourists, but it is surely one of the most historically significant. The Greek Orthodox Church is built over the only natural water source in Nazareth, and therefore it is almost certain that Mary would have regularly come here to fetch water, perhaps accompanied by her young son Jesus. Inside the church, there are steps leading down into a low vaulted cavern built by the Crusaders in the 12th century. Looking over the metal balustrade, the clear spring water can be seen. The Greek Orthodox Church believes it was here that the angel Gabriel

Left: The Old synagogue in Nazareth

Above: *The Church of St Joseph*

appeared to Mary, although this is without biblical support. Certainly Mary and her family would have been dependant upon this water spring. The town grew around this natural water supply.

The Old Synagogue

Not far from The Church of the Annunciation, there is a Crusader building known as 'The Old Synagogue'. Traditionally, this has been regarded as standing on the site of the original synagogue from the time when Jesus lived in Nazareth. The floor is believed to be even older than the building itself. Owned by the Greek Catholic Church, it is a simple structure, without any furnishings other than a few wooden seats. The simplicity of the building may be part of its attraction. Whether standing on the original site or not, it is a good place to stop and remember the beginning of Christ's public ministry. He came into the synagogue on the Sabbath day, and read from the scroll of Isaiah chapter 61 (Luke 4:16–21).

The Church of St Joseph

Beneath this church there are two caves that are said to have housed Joseph's workshop and a storage room. Today's visitor will only smell the sawdust from a modern carpenter's shop nearby! It has been suggested that Joseph may have been a stone mason rather than a carpenter, because limestone was commonly used for building. Either way, much of the traditional religious art depicting Jesus as a frail, fair-skinned young man is not at all accurate.

The remains of the Byzantine

Above: Gleaning the fields in the Nazareth Biblical Village

church include a small baptistry, clearly used only for babies during the latter part of the Byzantine era after most people had already converted to Christianity. The stained glass windows depict the angel's counsel to Joseph about marrying the already pregnant Mary; the betrothal of Joseph and Mary, with a ring being exchanged according to ancient Jewish custom; and the death of the ageing Joseph, with Mary and Jesus by his side.

Nazareth Biblical Village—A working reconstruction of the biblical village

A visit to Nazareth Village begins with a tour through four rooms full of information to enrich one's understanding of the history of Nazareth Village and the life and times of Jesus Christ. Based on thorough New Testament scholarship and the most up-to-date archaeology, Nazareth Village brings to life a farm and Galilean village, recreating Nazareth as it was 2,000 years ago. A winding path leads you through a working farm, past an ancient winepress and stone

Above: A woman at the well in Nazareth Biblical Village

quarries. On the hillside grape vines flourish and olive trees sway in the breeze. Donkeys pull a wooden plough and sheep graze on the hillside.

Each season brings new things to see as the farmer and villagers go about the tasks of that season: ploughing, planting, pruning, harvesting, threshing. The weaver and the carpenter demonstrate their crafts.

A Village guide describes Galilean life in the 1st century as visitors meet villagers dressed in 1st century costumes engaging in daily life activities in homes, in the olive press, and on the farm. One walks past cultivated terraces, an ancient winepress, a watchtower, stone quarries, grape vines, and old olive trees, and then enters a 1st century synagogue. The parables and teachings of Jesus come to life in this unique setting.

The Wedding Church in Cana

This church commemorates Jesus' first miracle, the changing of water into wine at the wedding in Cana (John 2). The large jugs of water referred to in the Scriptures were used for *netilat yadayim*, the Jewish ritual of washing and reciting a blessing before eating. Since all the Jewish guests at the wedding would have performed this ritual, large quantities of water were supplied. When a wedding took place during Jesus' time the entire village was invited, in addition to all the friends and relatives. The bride and the guests gathered at the home of her parents and awaited the groom, whose traditional late arrival caused tremendous tension to build up (Matthew 25). After the ceremony and celebration the wedding couple and their guests walked to the home of the groom's parents, taking the longest route through the village and making as much noise as possible. Once they arrived, they remained in their wedding clothes for a week while they held open house. Some families saved

Left: Khirbet Cana is on a hillside in the Netufa valley and many believe these are the ruins of the ancient village of Cana of Galilee

Above: *Mt Gerizim from Shechem*

for years in order to provide a wedding celebration for their daughters, and all the guests would discuss the particulars of the event the following day. For a family to run out of wine before the party was over would have been greatly humiliating: the potential disaster was prevented through the miracle by Jesus. It is significant that the first public miracle of Moses in the Old Testament was turning water into blood, a symbol of death (Exodus 7:14–25); but the first public miracle of Jesus was turning water into wine, a symbol of life and joy (John 2:1–11).

Samaria

The archaeological remains of Samaria are very impressive. The houses were built in Phoenician style and beautifully decorated. Archaeologists have found locally carved ivories that illustrate the prophets' reproach that in the time of Ahab the rich people of Samaria were living in houses of ivory (Amos 3:15;6:4).

Omri's son Ahab had sufficient capital to expand the city walls and build several temples, including one for Yahweh and another for the Phoenician god Baal, who was opposed by the prophet Elijah (1 Kings 18:18–40). The Samaritans were descendants of the foreigners from across the Assyrian empire who were settled in the land by Sargon in 722 BC to repopulate the northern kingdom after his destruction of Samaria in that year. The local population had been taken into exile. The Samaritans integrated their pagan beliefs with Judaism and accepted only the first five books of Moses (the Pentateuch); consequently they were always considered as 'heretics' by the Jews—hence the point of the parable of the Good Samaritan (Luke 10:30–37 and compare John 4:9).

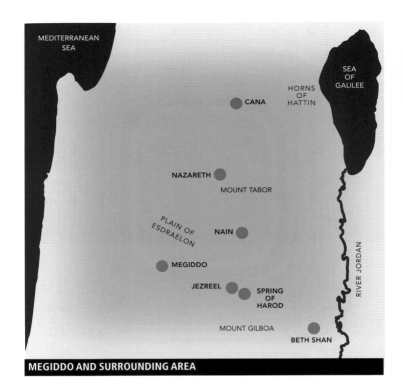

MEDITERRANEAN
SEA

SEA
OF
GALILEE

CANA

HORNS
OF
HATTIN

NAZARETH

MOUNT TABOR

PLAIN OF
ESDRAELON

NAIN

MEGIDDO

JEZREEL

SPRING
OF
HAROD

RIVER JORDAN

MOUNT GILBOA

BETH SHAN

MEGIDDO AND SURROUNDING AREA

TRAVEL INFORMATION

Unless otherwise noted most places in this travel section will be found on the websites: http://www.science.co.il/nature.asp OR www.sacred-destinations.com

Megiddo

(04) 6950316
Tel Megiddo National Park is on Route 66 between Megiddo junction and Yokne'am junction, about 2 kilometres northwest of Megiddo junction.

The 70m (230ft) water

Above: *A sweeping view across the Jezreel Valley*

tunnel is a must, providing you can walk down the staircase.

Open: April–September: 0800–1700; October–March: 0800–1600

Mount Carmel National Park

Take Route 4 to Oren junction and turn east From Route 70 turn west and at the city of

Left: A carpenter's workshop inside the Biblical Village

Nesher head towards the University of Haifa.

Open: April–September: 0800–1700; October–March: 0800–1600

Nazareth Village

Website: http://www.nazarethvillage.com/

Open 0900–1700 Monday through Saturday. Closed on Sundays. It is preferable to arrange a visit, although walk-ins are welcome. The last tour each day begins at 1500 hrs unless special arrangements are made.

For special requests for tours at other times, call ☏ 97246456042 and leave a message.

The fax number is 97246559295.

Reservations may be made up to one year in advance by calling ☏ 97246456042 or via email info.

Nazareth

For Nazareth generally, see http://www.nazarethinfo.org/2

The Church of St Gabriel (Mary's Well)

The crypt of this ornate 18th century church houses a 1st century spring of water believed to be the source of Mary's Well. The spring is connected to the site of the Well by an underground aqueduct.

The Church of the Annunciation

From the Church of St Gabriel, a narrow street winds among the houses of Old Nazareth to the Church of the Annunciation. The huge modern-day building, completed in 1966, is constructed over a cave traditionally believed by Roman Catholics to be the site of the Annunciation.

At noon, its gates close to the public. They reopen at 2, but only until 4:30, and in summer until 5:45. On Sundays, the church is open only for mass.

The Old Synagogue

Within the marketplace is the Synagogue Church, the site of the ancient synagogue where Jesus is thought to have begun his ministry. It stands adjacent to the Greek Catholic church.

The Church of St Joseph

Situated in the same complex as the Basilica of the Annunciation, this is traditionally believed to stand on the site of the original workshop of Joseph, and the home of Mary and Joseph. It contains ruins from 1st century Nazareth.

④ Controlling the land

Standing at the crossroads of the world, Isra
attracted the greedy gaze of others. It has sa
conflict and bloodshed than most other countries on earth.
However, on this narrow coastal strip a Zionist dream was
realised

Joppa/Jaffa

Joppa is mentioned in an Ancient Egyptian letter from 1470 BC. It was conquered by the Egyptian Pharaoh Tuthmosis III who, predating the exploits of Ali Baba (and the Trojan horse), hid armed warriors in large baskets and gave the baskets as a present to the city's governor. Upon delivery inside the city the soldiers appeared and overpowered the defenders. For many centuries Jaffa was the main port of entry into the land of Israel, and Jonah passed there on his way to Tarshish. Greek tradition records that the beautiful maiden, Andromeda, was once captured by a terrible sea monster at Jaffa and was rescued by the brave Perseus, who chopped up the monster and cast the pieces into the sea—those pieces are supposedly the rocks seen today not far off shore

The Bible records that this region was part of the allotment for the tribe of Dan (Joshua 19:46). Also, Hiram King of Tyre floated logs from Lebanon to Joppa for Solomon to use in Jerusalem (2 Chronicles 2:16). As did the people of Tyre and Sidon when ordered to by Cyrus the Great (Ezra 3:7). Jonah set

Facing page: An aerial view shows the ancient Herodian port of Caesarea

Above: The ancient city of Joppa was well known to both Jonah and Peter. Today it is called Jaffa

sail from here (Jonah 1:3) And Tabitha, also called Dorcas, lived here (Acts 9:36); Simon Peter was staying here by the Sea with Simon the Tanner (Acts 10:5), where Peter saw his vision of a large sheet full of animals here as well (Acts 11:5). Napoleon's storming of Jaffa in 1799 was particularly brutal when French soldiers bayoneted approximately 2,000 Turkish soldiers who were trying to surrender, and went on to murder men, women, and children and massacred 3,000 Turkish prisoners.

The city of Jaffa in the 19th century was walled, crowded and dirty. In the early 1900s, a handful of Jews living there decided to move outside its walls; they bought a plot of land covered by sand dunes, drew lots to distribute the land, and what was to become Tel Aviv was born in 1909. The name 'Tel Aviv' is the Hebrew translation of the German name Altneuland, a novel written by Theodore Herzl, the founder of modern Israel, and published in 1902 in Germany. In his novel he describes a Zionist utopia—a modern social-democratic Jewish State in which Arabs and Jews have equal rights. It was a far cry from the accusations that Herzl or the other leaders wanted to expel Arabs from Palestine. Herzl's ideal in The Jewish State (published in 1896) laid the plans for this utopia, while Altneuland gave it life. The founding of modern Tel Aviv was the fulfilment of Herzl's dream. A mixture of ancient and modern; a Tel, as we have seen, is an archaeological mound and aviv means spring. More and more garden neighbourhoods developed outside the walls, so that it was not long before Jaffa became a suburb of Tel Aviv. Today it is the largest city in Isarel. The section of Jaffa near the sea has been renovated, attracting Israelis and tourists alike to its restaurants, clubs and galleries.

Above: Tel Aviv is a modern city

The House of Simon the Tanner

High on a hill in old Jaffa, the Franciscan Monastery of Saint Peter is close to a narrow alley in which there is a mosque, built in 1730, the oldest in Jaffa. According to Christian tradition, on this site stood the house of Simon the tanner (Acts 10:5–32). No one can be sure if this really is the site. Peter fell asleep on the roof and received a vision of a sheet that came down from heaven, full of all kinds of animals, 'clean' and 'unclean'. In his vision, God spoke to him,

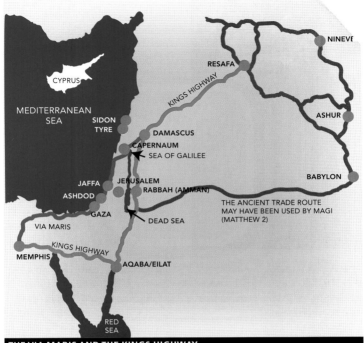

THE VIA MARIS AND THE KINGS HIGHWAY

Via Maris—'The Way of the Sea'

Two of the most important trade routes in the ancient world were the 'Kings Highway' running through Jordan from the Gulf of Aqaba to Damascus and Mesopotamia, and the 'Via Maris', the 'way of the sea' that ran along the Mediterranean coast from Egypt to the Lebanon and Syria. The 'Via Maris' was immensely strategic as a path that linked together the three continents of Africa, Asia and Europe. It is therefore significant that Jesus chose to begin his ministry in the coastal town of Capernaum that lay directly on this route, a meeting place for Jews and non-Jews, and 'launch-pad' for the Christian message. There is a standing stone among the ruins in Capernaum, with the inscription 'Via Maris'.

commanding Peter to eat from all the animals, despite the fact that some of them did not comply with the Jewish dietary laws. Peter had to learn that the message of Jesus was for all people, even for those who, as a Jew, he considered outside the covenant.

Caesarea

Caesarea began as a tiny fishing village on the coast of the Mediterranean Sea. It was transformed into a large port city around 22 BC by King Herod, who needed an outlet from which to export large quantities of

Above: Some critics of the Bible denied the existence of Pontius Pilate until this stone bearing his name was discovered in Caesarea

goods and produce to Rome. He built Caesarea after the pattern of a Roman city with all the required trappings: a theatre, amphitheatre, hippodrome, pagan temples, a palace and an elaborate aqueduct system. He named the city after Caesar Augustus (emperor of Rome from 27 BC to AD 14) who gave him the title of King. Pontius Pilate had his official residence here, as the headquarters of the Roman garrison in Palestine and Judea was in Caesarea.

In biblical history, Caesarea has been very significant. The deacon Philip settled here (Acts 8:40) and the apostle Paul stayed in his home on returning from his third missionary journey (Acts 21:8–9). It was here in Caesarea that a Roman centurion had a vision in which God told him to send for the apostle Peter (Acts 10:1–8). As a result, Cornelius and others in his household became Christians (Acts 10:23–28); through this, Peter understood that God's plan of salvation was not only for Jews but for Gentiles also. When Jerusalem was destroyed in the Jewish revolt

Above: An Aqueduct in Caesarea is a tribute to its Roman builders

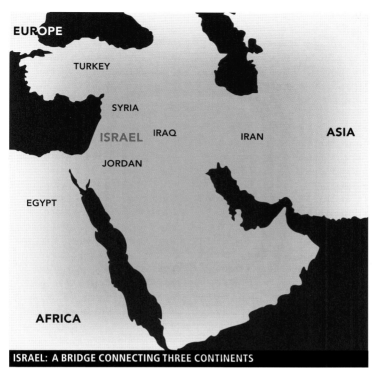

EUROPE

TURKEY

SYRIA

ISRAEL   IRAQ   IRAN   ASIA

JORDAN

EGYPT

AFRICA

ISRAEL: A BRIDGE CONNECTING THREE CONTINENTS

The Crusades in the Holy Land

By the close of the 11th century the Turks, followers of the religion of Islam, controlled territory that included what the church in the West thought of as 'The Holy Land'. Soon stories of the Turks attacking Christian pilgrims on their way to Jerusalem reached the West, and in addition the Byzantine church in the East appealed for help. Many in Europe felt that they should retain control of the Christian holy places. The first Crusade (the origin of the word can be traced to the cross embroidered garment worn by the 'crusaders') set out in 1095 and over the next 300 years eight or nine Crusades were fought in the 'Holy Land'. At the end of the last in 1272 the battle to retain Jerusalem was finally lost. By the end of that century the religious Crusades were over, and when the last cities fell, the Christian inhabitants were either massacred, sold into slavery or forced to convert. Throughout those centuries, the bitter fighting, broken alliances and cruel slaughter on both sides brought no credit either to Islam or Christianity.

of AD 70, the Romans made Caesarea their administrative capital. The Byzantine Christians kept the city flourishing, but closed down public places where the activities were regarded as morally wrong—such as the Roman theatre. The city changed hands a number of times during the Crusades. It was eventually lost to the Muslims, who abandoned it. Bosnians, serving as land administration clerks for the Ottoman Turks, moved in during the mid 1800s but fled during the Israeli War of Independence. Since then, the city has been under the jurisdiction of the national parks authority and is still being excavated.

The following places are worth noting in Caesarea:

The Theatre

A stone bearing the name 'Pontius Pilate' was found here at the theatre. A replica is now on display there and the original is in the Israel Museum in Jerusalem. The theatre was excavated from the sands of Caesarea during 1959. The seating area, or cavea, originally held 3,500 spectators, with a special VIP section in the 'orchestra,' no doubt reserved for Herod and his guests. Later the floor here was covered with marble and filled with water to enable the re-enactment of famous sea battles.

The Crusader Gate

The fortifications of Caesarea built by the Crusaders are in excellent condition in many places, enabling us to understand how they defended the city. The high, sloped walls were surrounded by a deep moat which was always dry despite the nearby water because of the site's slight elevation above sea level. A wooden drawbridge spanned the moat at the city's entry gate. For the Crusaders, Caesarea was an important link in their chain of fortresses and ports along the coastal plain. However, once the Muslims had defeated the Crusaders, the city held no value for them and they abandoned it to the sands.

Above: *The Apostle Paul was imprisoned at Herod's harbour in Caesarea*

Above: The world headquarters of the Bahai religion overlooks Haifa Bay

The Herodian Port

Caesarea lacked two most important requirements: a port with deep water near the shore, and an inlet to protect the ships. In order to create the necessary conditions Herod used cement, which the Romans had found would harden under water, moulding a great horseshoe shaped wall beneath the waves, on top of which he mounted huge 'jacks' which served as wave breakers. Two towers along the wall guarded the port and controlled traffic entering and leaving. Unfortunately, Herod's undersea wall was destroyed not long after his death by an earthquake at sea.

Herod's palace at Caesarea is another example of one man's mania for difficult building challenges. The palace was built on a small peninsula jutting out into the sea and surrounded on three sides by water. The central court contained a large open-air swimming pool with fountains that would have been most logically filled with the easily accessible sea water; however, excavators have uncovered a series of pipes indicating that Herod insisted on filling the pool with fresh water brought from the shore despite the inconvenience.

Haifa

Haifa was inhabited by the ancient Phoenicians as well as by Greeks and Jews, but it was destroyed by the Muslims in the 7th century. Rebuilt by the Crusaders it was later destroyed again and not until the 20th century did the city revive and expand. The British constructed a harbour here in 1929 and turned Haifa into the trading and commercial centre of Israel. Under British rule, more than a million and a half immigrant Jews disembarked here; falling on the land at Haifa's docks, they kissed the ground of their Promised Land as they began their new life in Israel. Haifa is also the international centre for the Bahai religion, a religion founded in late 19th century Persia. Originally an offshoot of Shiite Islam, today the Bahai's are an independent religious group. One of its founders, the Bahaula, was exiled to Palestine from Persia and subsequently died in Haifa. His gold-domed tomb, on the slopes of Carmel, is an important shrine of the Bahai's, for whom Haifa is a holy city. Their international centre, a huge expensive building surrounded by acres of carefully manicured gardens, is just above the burial shrine.

Mount Carmel

Haifa is located on the slopes of Mount Carmel, on the Mediterranean Sea, and is Israel's third largest city. It is built on three levels, the lower level ('downtown') being the port area with shipping companies, small businesses and warehouses; this is not the best part of the city. The second level is 'Hadar', mid-way up Carmel, and the business centre of town. The top level, 'Carmel', is the most attractive part of the city, especially for the visitor.

Mount Carmel was the site of an abandoned altar to Yahweh (1 Kings 18:30). The prophet Elijah chose this place, overlooking the Jezreel Valley, for his courageous conflict

Above: A stained glass window in the Carmelite monastery on Mount Carmel shows Elijah ascending in a fiery chariot

Above: Here on Mount Carmel Elijah faced the prophets of Baal

with the false prophets of Baal (1 Kings 18:19–39). When the 450 prophets of Baal were defeated by God's prophet Elijah, they were taken to the Brook Kishon at the foot of the mountain and killed (1 Kings 18:40). A little further east is a cave just beneath the Stella Maris monastery, which is traditionally regarded as the place to which Elijah fled, although the Bible records his flight south to Horeb (1 Kings 19:9).

Further north is the town of Acre, and if the visibility is clear

Above: The architecture of Acre is a reminder that it once served as a Crusader port

you can see Rosh HaNikra, the White Sea grottos on Israel's western-most border with Lebanon.

Acre

Acre (also spelt Acco or Akko) is the only remaining 'live' Crusader town in Israel. It is a 4000 year-old seaport, with a troubled past. Conquered at one time by Egyptian Pharaohs, Acre became the capital city of one of the ten tribes of Israel, Asher—although the tribe never actually defeated it (Judges 1:31). It became a part of Israel under the reigns of David and Solomon. However, Acre was given back to the Phoenicians as payment to King Hiram, in exchange for the men and materials he provided to help in building Jerusalem (1 Kings 9:11–13; 2 Chronicles 8:1–2).

Alexander the Great took over Acre following his conquest of Tyre, and its name was changed to Ptolemais.

Above: There are extensive ancient ruins in Beth Shean, which was one of the great cities of the Decapolis

Claudius, Roman emperor from AD 41–54, made it a colony. When the Crusaders arrived in 1104, they made Acre the main port of the Holy Land. Napoleon unsuccessfully attacked the city in 1799, thereby dashing his hopes for an eastern empire. Instead of this, the Muslim ruler 'el-Jezzar' fortified the city to make it his stronghold, building its huge mosque and luxurious steam baths. Such was his cruelty, that he was known as 'the Butcher of Acre'.

Today Acre is a bustling modern city. However, for Christian visitors it is more than simply a historic place with medieval character. It was the most important seaport in Israel throughout the centuries, including the period of the early church. In the New Testament,

Luke writes: 'And when we had finished our voyage from Tyre, we came to Ptolemais, greeted the brethren, and stayed with them one day' (Acts 21:7). This is Acre—a seaport, a stronghold through the ages, and a stopping place for Christian travellers.

Beth Shean (or Shan)

Called Israel's Pompeii, the settlement of Beit Shean began in the 5th century BC on a hilltop in the heart of a fertile area with plenty of water, and at the crossroads of major thoroughfares. It was part of the allotment of Manasseh after the conquest of the land (Joshua 17:11). However they did not drive out the inhabitants (Judges 1:27). During the late Canaanite period (16th to 12th centuries BC), it was the seat of Egyptian rule in Israel. After the battle on nearby Mount Gilboa, the Philistines hung the bodies of King Saul and his sons on the city walls (1 Samuel 31:10). King David seems to have captured Beth Shean together with Megiddo and Taanach, and during King Solomon's reign the city was included in the administrative district of the valleys (1 Kings 4:12). Beth Shean was destroyed in 732 BC when Tiglath Pileser III, King of Assyria, captured the northern part of Israel. Beth Shean was one of the ten federated cities known as the Decapolis alliance and the most important city in northern Israel. The ruin mound (tel) now stands over 75m (240ft) high composed of the evidence of eighteen generations of occupants.

Spring of Harod (Ein Harod)

The Spring of Harod bubbles in a cave on the slopes of Mount Gilboa. The clear water flows in a brook through the grassy Harod Spring National Park en route to its final destination: the Jezreel Valley farms.

The cave is called Gideon's Cave, based on the story in Judges 7. It was very likely this spring at which Gideon tested his soldiers by asking them to drink (Judges 7:5–7).

The nearby Gan Hashlosha National Park has springs, natural pools, and naturally warm water.

Belvoir

This Crusader fortress is located 19km (12mi) south of the Sea of Galilee. It overlooks the winding Jordan River below and faces the hills of Gilead. It was named Belvoir (Fair View) by the Crusaders. After the victory of the Muslim army under Saladin over the Crusaders at the battle of the Horns of Hattin, Belvoir was besieged. The siege lasted a year and a half, until the defenders surrendered on 5 January 1189.

The fortifications of Belvoir were dismantled in 1217–18 by the Muslim rulers who feared the re-conquest of the fortress by the Crusaders. It is the most complete and impressive Crusader fortress in Israel and stands as a reminder of a violent and cruel period.

Above: Mount Gilboa was very familiar to Gideon, one of the Old Testament Judges

Above: Ein Harod is also known as Gideon's Spring

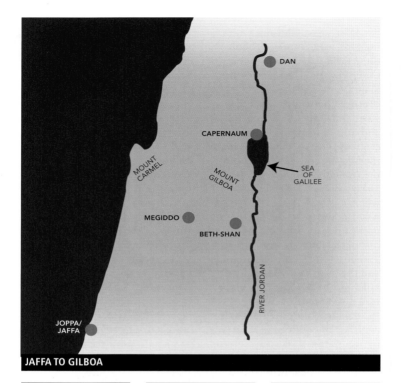

DAN

CAPERNAUM

MOUNT CARMEL

MOUNT OF GILBOA

SEA OF GALILEE

MEGIDDO

BETH-SHAN

RIVER JORDAN

JOPPA/ JAFFA

JAFFA TO GILBOA

TRAVEL INFORMATION

Unless otherwise noted most places in this travel section will be found on the websites: http://www. science.co.il/nature. asp OR www.sacred-destinations.com

Beth Shean

(04) 6587189
   The Beth Shean National Park is situated in the city of Beit She'an (or Bethshan). Signs at the entrances to Beit Shean direct visitors to the antiquities.

Spring of Harod

04–653222211 Fax: 04–655531136
   The Israel Nature and Parks Authority and the Gilboa Regional Council have carried out large-scale development work in the park. Visitors will find lawns, shady trees, a swimming pool, sports and play equipment, a dressing room, and toilets. Groups may stay overnight by prior arrangement. The nearby Ma'ayan Harod Youth Hostel offers air-conditioned family accommodation with showers and toilets in

Right: A remaining archway reflects the former glory of the Crusader fortress of Belvoir

Left: Herod's swimming pool in Caesarea was originally filled with fresh water brought in by a system of pipes

each unit. At the western end of the park is a 6,000 seat amphitheatre.

Harod Spring Nature Reserve is on Route 71 between Afula and Beit Shan. Six miles from Afula, turn in the direction of Gideona. Another option is to take Route 675 from Hasargel junction to Navot junction; the entrance to the national park is just a half-mile past the junction.

Open: April–September: 0800–1700. July–August: 0800–1800. October–March: 0800–1600

Gan Hashlosha National Park

✆ (04) 6586219

Gan Hashlosha National Park is well worth a visit. Since its water is 28°C summer and winter, visitors can swim in the river all year round. The water collects in a natural pool with freshwater fish. The river banks have well tended lawns and a landscaped garden with beautiful flowers and foliage.

The park also has, lifeguards, showers, restaurant, snack bar, archaeological museum, tower-and-stockade museum, flour mill, gym, pool, shaded areas, picnic tables, playground and water slides. The park is wheelchair accessible.

Belvoir

Remained in ruins until comprehensive excavations were conducted in 1966. The site was then opened to visitors.

Caesarea National Park

✆ (04) 6267080

Directions: Caesarea National Park is on the coastal road near the city of Caesarea and Kibbutz Sdot Yam and west of Or Akiva. Take the coastal road or the old Tel Aviv-Haifa highway to the interchange near the Orot Rabin power station; an alternative route is to drive to the park via Or Akiva.

Open: April–September: 0800–1700; October–March: 0800–1600

Mount Carmel National Park

✆ (04) 8231452 or (04) 9841750

Directions: To get to the Mount Carmel National Park, take Route 4 (the old Tel Aviv-Haifa highway) to Oren junction and turn east from Route 70 (Faradis-Yokne'am), turn west to the Eliakim interchange and at the city of Nesher, head towards the University of Haifa. Open all year.

⑤ Dead or alive

In a small chapel in the Church of the Nativity is a marble floor with an inlaid silver star surrounded by a simple Latin inscription announcing the most astonishing event in history: 'Here Jesus Christ was born of the virgin Mary'

Bethlehem

On the main road, just before the turning to Bethlehem, is Rachel's Tomb, the traditional burial site of the biblical matriarch who died after giving birth to Benjamin (Genesis 35:19). Bethlehem is where Ruth of Moab returned with Naomi to live and where she gleaned the fields (Ruth 1 and 2). It is also where David was anointed king by Samuel (1 Sam. 16:4–13), and it was from the well of Bethlehem that three of David's warriors brought him water when he was hiding in the cave of Adullam (2 Sam. 23:13–17). Most important of all are the events connected with the birth of Jesus, and the visit of the wise men.

The Church of the Nativity

This church was first built in the 4th century AD by Helena, the mother of the Roman Emperor Constantine. Bethlehem is formed from the Hebrew words *beit lehem*, meaning 'house of bread'. The name indicates that Bethlehem has always been an agricultural community, with most of its residents earning their livelihood from farming and shepherding. The fertile valleys were used for raising crops, while the rocky hills were more suitable for grazing. The limestone rock on which Bethlehem is built is susceptible to a chemical process that occurs when water comes into contact with limestone, causing the rock to dissolve. This phenomenon has formed hundreds of natural caves in the hills of Bethlehem which have been used for centuries by

Facing page: Qumran was home to a religious group during Bible times called the Essenes

Above: *A large mosque faces onto Manger Square in Bethlehem*

Right: *According to Christian tradition John the Baptist was born in Ein Karem near Bethlehem as commemorated at the Church of the Visitation*

shepherds to protect their flocks from the summer heat and the winter rains.

The Shepherds' Fields

When Mary and Joseph arrived in Bethlehem and found no room at the inn, it is likely that they went to a cave at the edge of the village which was used by local shepherds to water and feed their flocks; the manger was literally 'a feeding trough'. Whether or not the identified cave is the one in which Jesus was born is impossible to say, but certainly the Grotto of the Nativity is the only claimant. This is a good place to remember the shepherds 'living out in the fields' because it is out in open country, far removed from the hustle and bustle of the city of Bethlehem (Luke 2:1–20).

Bethany

Bethany is a village east of Jerusalem on the road to Jericho, called in Arabic El Azarieh. This is where Jesus raised Lazarus from the dead (John 11). Christian

Above: *The small door into the Church of the Nativity in Bethlehem has a story to tell*

tradition identifies the Lazarus Tomb. Similarly, a church is built upon the traditional site of the home of Mary, Martha and Lazarus (Luke 10:38). There can be no certainty for either of these sites, although it is a delightful village to visit and recall those events in the life of Jesus Christ.

On the road to the Dead Sea

Jesus told a parable about a certain man who 'went down from Jerusalem to Jericho' (Luke 10:30–37). Glancing at a map of Israel, the word 'down' seems like a mistake, as Jericho is actually 27km (17mi) northeast of Jerusalem. However, Jerusalem is 825m (2700ft) above sea level, while Jericho itself is 260m (850ft) below sea level. So the drive from Jerusalem to Jericho involves a drop of nearly 1100m (3600ft).

Along the road many Bedouin camps are visible. The Bedouin are traditionally a nomadic people who wandered through the desert and stopped wherever they could graze their flocks and find water. Located on the road is the Inn of the Good Samaritan. Although the story of the Good Samaritan was a parable told by Jesus rather than an actual event, he and his hearers would have been familiar with inns like this.

Jericho

Jericho became known as 'the city of palm trees' (Deuteronomy 34:3). All that now remains of Old Testament Jericho is the large mound, Tel Jericho, measuring 365m (1200ft) long and 15m (50ft) high; it is famous as the first city captured by the Israelites under Joshua. Rahab the prostitute lived here and Joshua sent spies to assess the city's strength (Joshua 2:1–15); this walled city was the first line of defence for

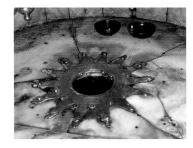

Above: In the crypt of the Church of the Nativity in Bethlehem a star marks the traditional site of Jesus birthplace

Below: Modern Bethlehem stands alongside the Shepherds Fields

Above: Bethany where Jesus spent time with Mary Martha and their brother Lazarus

the Canaanites (Joshua 6:1–17). But Joshua trusted God, and saw the walls come tumbling down (Joshua 6:20).

A series of archaeological digs was carried out at old Jericho, most notably by Professor John Garstang and Dame Kathleen Kenyon. Garstang's excavations offered a date of around 1377 BC for the fall of Jericho, (Joshua 6:20, 24). He also discovered Egyptian scarabs that bear the names of Hatshepsut, Tuthmosis III and Amenhophis II, which tie in with a 15th century BC date for

Below: The wall that separates Bethlehem from Jerusalem is a heartache to both Jews and Arabs

the Exodus. Garstang believed he had found the burnt walls of the city destroyed by Joshua, though Kenyon disputed this and the debate continues. Ancient Tel Jericho is one mile from the present day city.

Jericho was an ideal place for settlement. The Spring of Elisha, situated at the foot of the Tel, provides an average outflow of 170 litres/sec (2000 gallons/min) all year round. This is the water that Elisha the prophet made pure (2 Kings 2:19–22); it is the life stream of the city. In addition, Tel Jericho directly overlooks the ancient highway to the north, making it a very strategic position both commercially and militarily.

Behind Tel Jericho is the Mount and Monastery of Temptation. According to tradition, Jesus came to this spot in the wilderness where he was tempted by the devil and 'taken up on a high mountain' (Luke 4:1–13). In Jesus' day a new centre had been constructed on the wadi banks in the foreground, by the Hasmonean rulers, and by Herod the Great who turned it

Above: An old Turkish police station is today called The Good Samaritan Inn

into a lovely place. It was here in the new Jericho that Zacchaeus climbed a tree to see Jesus (Luke 19:1–10); here also Jesus healed blind Bartimaeus (Mark 10:46–52).

Ein Gedi (biblical En Gedi)

Ein Gedi, the western coast of the Dead Sea, is an oasis in the desert. The name Ein Gedi means 'spring of the goat'; it is a natural spring which emerges between the cliffs and serves as a watering hole for desert wildlife, including hyrax, ibex, hyena and leopard. It was given as part of Judah's inheritance (Joshua 15:62) and was known as Hazazon Tamar (2 Chronicles 20:2). However, it is best known as David's stronghold (1 Samuel 24), a place of safety when he hid from Saul. The cliffs are peppered with caves, and in one of these caves David spared King Saul after cutting off a piece of his tunic.

Masada

Rising above the shores of the Dead Sea, Masada (Hebrew for 'fortress') is situated on top of an isolated rock cliff at the western end of the Judean desert, overlooking the Dead Sea. On the east, the rock falls in a sheer drop of 1470m (450ft) to the Dead Sea, and in the west it stands 1076m (328ft) above the surrounding terrain. The natural approaches

Below: The walls of Jericho came tumbling down and the evidence can be seen today

The Dead Sea

The Dead Sea has had many names. The Hebrews called it 'The Salt Sea' (Genesis 14:3); the Greeks preferred 'Asphalt Sea' because of its chemical properties. Jerome in the 4th century called it the 'Dead Sea' because nothing can live in it; the Arabs simply called it 'The Sea of Lot' because this area is associated with Abraham's nephew (Genesis 13:10–13).

The Dead Sea is a large (though rapidly shrinking) salt lake lying inside a huge crack in the earth's crust called the Syrian African Rift. This rift valley runs from Damascus, through Israel and Jordan, to Lake Victoria in Africa. The Dead Sea is in the deepest part of the valley, which makes it the lowest point on earth at 400m (1320ft) below sea level. The Sea of Galilee is also inside the valley, but is only 200m (656ft) below sea level. The water of the Dead Sea is so salty that it cannot support life or be used for irrigation or drinking. While the average ocean is 2–3% salts, the Dead Sea is 32% salts. However, the waters of the Dead Sea have long been recognized for their special concentration of minerals. The most significant product is potash, used in chemical fertilizers and exported all over the world. The Dead Sea is also well-known for its curative properties, particularly for skin diseases and joint ailments.

to the cliff top are very difficult. Separated from the mountain range by two deep wadis (a wadi is a watercourse that runs dry in the summer), Masada was a natural fortress. In the years 37–4 BC, King Herod further fortified Masada and turned it into a luxurious mountain resort with steam baths, water cisterns, guard towers, weapons and food storehouses for possible refuge were he to be overthrown.

In AD 66, during the Jewish

Above: *Saint George's Monastery is located on the near vertical slope of a deep canyon in the Judean Desert between Jerusalem and Jericho*

revolt against the Romans, Masada was captured by a small group of Jewish Zealots. They and other refugee families remained there even after the fall of Jerusalem and the destruction of the Temple in AD 70. However, in AD 72 the Roman General Silva decided to put an end to the tiniest pockets of resistance against Rome. He built a wall around the base of the mountain and established eight siege camps to prevent escape; on the western side he built a siege ramp. The Jews of Masada preferred death by their own hands rather than slavery and possible execution at the hands of the Romans, therefore the men killed their wives and children, and then each other. When the Romans finally scaled the heights and broke in, they were met by the eerie silence of 960 corpses.

Today, Masada is one of the Jewish people's greatest symbols. Israeli soldiers take an oath here: 'Masada shall not fall again.' Next to Jerusalem, it is the most popular destination of Jewish tourists visiting Israel.

Above: An aerial view shows Masada hanging on three levels on a desert mountain. It was built by Herod as a winter palace

Herodian (or Herodium)

Just south of Jerusalem, a huge volcano-like mound is visible for miles around. Herodian is a circular palace fortress built on top of a man-made hill, which rises 60m (200ft) above its surroundings. It was another massive building project by Herod, requiring a colossal quantity of earth to be heaped up, forming the base for a palace on a similar scale to Masada. Around the foot of the mound, Herod built smaller palaces, pools and terraced gardens.

Hebron

Hebron is mentioned eighty-seven times in the Bible, and Numbers 13:22 states that Hebron was founded seven years before the Egyptian town of Zoan; that places it around 1720 BC. Hebron is the site of the oldest Jewish community in the world. The city's history has been inseparably linked with the Cave of Machpelah, which the Patriarch Abraham purchased as a family tomb from Ephron the Hittite for 400 silver shekels (Genesis 23). As recorded in Genesis, the Patriarchs Abraham, Isaac, and Jacob, and the Matriarchs Sarah, Rebekah and Leah, are buried there. According to a Jewish tradition, Adam and Eve are also buried there.

Joshua assigned Hebron to Caleb from the tribe of

Qumran and the Dead Sea Scrolls

Qumran is 16km (10mi) south of Jericho, on the northwest coast of the Dead Sea. It was probably the home of the sect known as the 'Essenes', a monastic community of Jews who refused to conform to the Judaism practiced by the Pharisees and Sadducees; however, the precise identity of the occupants of Qumran is still a matter of debate. Despite claims to the contrary, there is no evidence that either John the Baptist or Jesus were influenced by the Essenes. With the Roman armies advancing in AD 68, the Essenes fled, hiding their scrolls in nearby caves where they remained for almost 2000 years.

In 1947 a Bedouin shepherd discovered the first of the Dead Sea Scrolls. Almost 1,000 scrolls were subsequently discovered in 11 caves and of these around two hundred are copies of biblical books with thirty copies of Deuteronomy alone. They were ultimately purchased by the Hebrew University of Jerusalem.

The Dead Sea Scrolls are dated between 200 BC and AD 100. Prior to their discovery, the earliest existing Old Testament manuscripts were dated AD 900 (the Masoretic texts), therefore the Dead Sea Scrolls were written about 1000 years earlier than these. Significantly, the differences between the Dead Sea and Masoretic texts are comparatively slight, indicating the extreme care with which the biblical texts were copied from generation to generation. A special museum was built to house these scrolls, called 'The Shrine of The Book' which is situated at the Israel Museum in Jerusalem (See The Shrine of the Book. Ch. 8).

Judah (Joshua 14:13–14), who subsequently led his tribe in

Above: En Gedi resort is a beautiful place from which to venture into the Dead Sea

conquering the city and its environs (Judges 1:1–20). Joshua 14:15 notes that 'the name of Hebron formerly was Kirjath Arba' because Arba was the greatest man among the Anakim. Following the death of King Saul, God instructed David to go to Hebron, where he was anointed King of Judah (2 Samuel 2:1–4), and a few years later David was anointed King over all Israel in Hebron (2 Samuel 5:1–3). The city fell to the Babylonians in 586 BC, but despite the loss of Jewish independence, Jews continued to live in Hebron (Nehemiah 11:25).

Lachish

Lachish is first mentioned in the Bible when Joshua destroyed

Above: *Hebron was the birthplace of Rachel in the Old Testament*

the city (Joshua 10:22–32). King David developed the city, and his grandson Rehoboam fortified it so that it became the second most important city in Judah after Jerusalem (2 Chronicles 11:5–11). King Amaziah fled to Lachish when a rebellion broke out in Jerusalem, but he was pursued and killed (2 Kings 14:1). Because of its strategic importance, the Assyrian King Sennacherib conquered Lachish in 701 BC and his victory was displayed on carved reliefs in his new palace in Nineveh; they are now in the British Museum in London. Thousands died in that battle: a mass grave has been found with 1500 skeletons, mainly of women and children, mixed with pottery from the year 701 BC. From the next siege, this time by the Babylonians under Nebuchadnezzar in 587 BC, eighteen Hebrew ostraca (pottery shards) were recovered. They are known as the Lachish letters.

Above: *The ancient city of Lachish is rich with history*

According to the prophet Jeremiah, Lachish and Azekah were the last two Judean cities to fall before the conquest of Jerusalem in 586 BC (Jeremiah 34:7). After the seventy-year exile in Babylon, some Jews returned to Lachish (Nehemiah 11:30).

Above: *David gained his victory over Goliath in the Valley of Elah*

Above: *The route from Jerusalem to Beersheba goes through the Negev Desert*

Gath

The Philistine city of Gath was located near Israelite territory at the end of the Elah Valley. The name of the city in Hebrew is *gat*, which means 'winepress'. Recent excavations uncovered a 2·5km (1·5mi) long moat that surrounded the city on three sides. This moat dates to the 9th century BC, and was apparently built by Hazael and his Aramean army when they were besieging the city in 811 BC (2 Kings 12:17). The most famous inhabitant of Gath was Goliath, the giant who fought David. After King Saul killed himself, David lamented: 'Tell it not in Gath' (2 Samuel 1:20)—a phrase that has become common in the English speaking world for keeping bad news silent.

Valley of Elah

The Valley of Elah is famous for one battle described in 1 Samuel 17. The Philistines camped between the cities of Socoh and Azekah. In response, Saul and the Israelite army moved into a defensive position on the northern ridge overlooking the Philistine camp. David made

the 24km (15mi) trek from his hometown of Bethlehem down to the Israelite camp in the Valley of Elah to bring provisions to his three older brothers. Obtaining permission from King Saul, David entered the valley, gathered five smooth stones from the bed of the seasonal stream, and killed Goliath. Seeing the giant lying dead, the Israelite forces swarmed down the hillside into the valley, chasing the Philistines westward through the Valley of Elah and pursuing them 11km (7mi) as far as Ekron.

Ashdod

About 6·5km (4mi) south of the present city is Tel Ashdod, another of the major Philistine cities and the site of the biblical city that was allocated to the tribe of Judah (Joshua 15:47). Ashdod was an important city because of its location along the coastal route leading from Egypt to Syria and Mesopotamia. The Philistines made the mistake of capturing the Ark of the Covenant and bringing it to Ashdod, where the community was struck by a

Above: The ancient Biblical site of Tel Sheva is now a National Archaeological Park

number of calamities that led the Philistines to return the Ark to Israel (1 Samuel 5).

Ashkelon

This was one of five Philistine city-states (along with Gath, Gaza, Ekron and Ashdod). Ashkelon was also a great trading centre because it lay along the Via Maris, the route linking Egypt with Syria and Mesopotamia. The city was conquered by the Philistines in the second half of the 12th century BC. After David defeated the Philistines he could not dislodge them from Ashkelon. This was finally accomplished by the Assyrian conqueror Tiglath-Pileser III in 734 BC. After roughly 600 years in the region, the Philistines disappeared for ever. It is believed that Ashkelon was the birthplace of Herod the Great in 37 BC. Archaeologists have unearthed a large cemetery for dogs in Ashkelon, though no one knows the significance of this! Also, a bronze and silver calf was discovered that is more than 3,500 years old and may be related to Baal worship.

Gaza

Gaza is one of the oldest cities in the world, mentioned specifically by name very early in the Bible (Genesis 10:19). Gaza was allotted to the tribe of Judah (Joshua 15:47). It was one of the five major Philistine cities that each gave a sin offering to stop the plague God inflicted upon them for their capture of the Ark of the Covenant (1 Samuel 5:1–6, 6:1–2, 6:17). After his betrayal by Delilah, Samson was blinded and taken prisoner to Gaza (Judges 16:21). It was there that he and 3,000 Philistines perished when he pulled down the pillars of the Philistine temple (Judges 16:25–30).

Gaza marked the border of the Israelite kingdom (1 Kings 4:24), and Hezekiah defeated the Philistines as far as Gaza in his efforts to re-establish Judah's independence (2 Kings 18:5–8). The prophet Jeremiah spoke of Gaza's devastation by the Egyptians (Jeremiah 47:1–5), and the prophets Amos and Zephaniah also warned of its destruction (Amos 1:6–7, Zephaniah 2:4).

Beersheba

Beersheba (also spelt Beer-Sheva) lies 45km (28mi) southwest of Hebron and is regarded as the gateway to the Negev desert. The name Beersheba means 'the well of seven' or 'the well of the oath.' It was here that Abraham and Abimelech, King of Gerar, pledged mutual allegiance (Genesis 21:31). Traditionally, Beersheba has not only been the southern border of Judah's territory (Joshua 25:28; Judges 10:1; 1 Samuel 3:20) but the southern border of the Promised Land itself, as the expression 'from Dan to Beersheba' suggests.

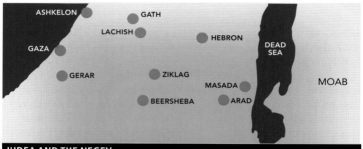

JUDEA AND THE NEGEV

TRAVEL INFORMATION

Unless otherwise noted most places in this travel section will be found on the websites: http://www.science.co.il/nature.asp OR www.sacred-destinations.com

Masada

📞 086584207/8

The ascent of Masada generally begins at the Visitors' Centre. There are two options: a forty five minute walk to the summit via the winding snake path, or a ten minute cable car ride. Either way, the summit affords glorious views of the Judean Desert, the Dead Sea, and the mountains of Moab in Jordan. The story of the last stand of the Jews of Masada is also told by an audio-visual show, which takes place between March and October, on Tuesdays and Thursdays.

Open: April–September 0800–1700; October–March 0800–1600. On Fridays and holiday evenings closing time is one hour earlier. The cable train works on Sunday–Thursday & Saturday 0800–1600.

Qumran National Park

📞 (02) 9942235

Directions: Qumran National Park is off of Route 90 near Kibbutz Kalia, north of the Dead Sea. The park is about a 40–minute drive from Jerusalem.

Open: April–September 0800–1700; October–March 0800–1600

Note: The Dead Sea Scrolls are kept at The Shrine of the Book, which is part of The Israel Museum in Jerusalem (www.imj.org.il)

Left: The extensive ruins of Masada recall the Jewish Zealots' last stand against the Romans

Ein Gedi Nature Reserve

📞 (07) 6584285

Like a huge oasis near the Dead Sea, the 2530 hectare (6,250 acre) reserve sits on the Syrian-African Rift. It is watered by four natural springs: David, Arugot, Shulamit, and Ein Gedi. These ensure a wealth of flora and fauna—a stark contrast to the parched desert all around.

Directions: The Ein Gedi Nature Reserve is on Route 90 (Dead Sea road) about 1 kilometre north of Kibbutz Ein Gedi.

Open: April–September 0800–1700; October–March 0800–1600

Herodion National Park

Herodion National Park is near Nokdiim and Tekoa. From Jerusalem take Route 356 at Gilo junction past Har Homa to Tekoa and Herodion.

Open: April–September 0800–1700; October–March 0800–1600

Lachish

The site was last excavated in the eighties and as it has not been turned into a national park, it is rather overgrown; helpful signs or explanations are absent. To reach Lachish: take the Bet Shemesh road south in the direction of Kiryat Gat. Turn south onto route 3415 till reaching the car park.

Ashkelon: The National Park

This is the site in Ashkelon of the ancient city. It is located on the southern coast of modern Ashkelon. From the entrance the road passes through the 12th century Crusader city walls and the Canaanite earth ramparts. There are several ongoing excavation sites near the sea, which reveal the city's biblical roots. One of the most intriguing sections of the park is the sculpture garden,

in which many Roman statues stand. There are also several ruins of Byzantine and Crusader churches within the Park.

Tel Beersheva National Park

📞 (08) 6467286

Directions: Tel Beersheva National Park is on the Beersheva-Shokat junction road, south of the city of Omer and near the Bedouin settlement of Tel Sheva. The park is a 10–minute drive from Beersheva.

Open: April–September 0800–1700; October–March 0800–1600

Hebron

Hebron (Al-Khalil in Arabic) is located 32km (20 mi) south of Jerusalem in the Judean hills, and sits between 870 and 1020m (2850 and 3350ft) above sea level. The city is built on several hills and wadis. Its monthly average temperatures are lower than those of Jerusalem.

During its long and trou
attacked on more than f
seven times. After three
still caught up in the st
Ironically this is a city

time of Ezra and Nehemi
This marks the beginni
Second Temple peri
includes the rebui
Temple by Kin
latter half of
When the
Alexan
the P

A Short History of Jerusalem

The history of Jerusalem begins at the lower ridge called Zion, just south of the Temple Mount. Canaanites settled here 5000 years ago. It was a strategic place because it is surrounded by valleys on three sides: the Kidron on the east, the Valley of Hinnom on the South and the Tyropoeon Valley on the west. There is no valley on the northern side however, so this has always been the most vulnerable part of Jerusalem. Of the thirty-seven times the city of Jerusalem has been conquered, on all but two it was taken from the north; the two exceptions were King David in 1000 BC, who probably climbed up through the water system on the eastern side, and the Israel Defence Forces in the Six Day War in 1967, who entered the city through the Lions' Gate, also in the east

When the Israelites captured the Promised Land under the leadership of Joshua around 1400 BC, the city was occupied by a Canaanite people called the Jebusites (Judges 19:10–12). When King David succeeded Saul to the throne of Israel, they had still not been conquered and David, wishing to unite the twelve tribes under one king and one

cap...
because it was enemy te... ...
David further strengthened the status of Jerusalem by settling the Ark of the Covenant there. The responsibility for building the Temple fell to his son Solomon.

Solomon's Temple is known as the First Temple and it stood from 950 until 586 BC. The First Temple Period ended with the destruction of the Temple, the city and the exile of the Jewish people to Babylon. When the Persians conquered the Babylonians, the Persian King Cyrus invited the Jews to return to Jerusalem and rebuild the Temple, a task which was completed in 516 BC in the

Facing page: Modern Jerusalem retains its ancient history

Above: *Visitors to Capernaum will see a carving of the Ark of the Covenant among the stone ruins*

h.
ng of the
d, which
ding of the
Herod in the
the 1st century BC.
Macedonian ruler
der the Great conquered
rsian Empire, Jerusalem fell
der his control. At his death it
passed to the Egyptian Ptolemaic
dynasty and in 198 BC the Syrians
entered Palestine. By 142 BC the
Maccabean wars had resulted
in Jewish independence and the
establishment of the Hasmonean
Kingdom. By the middle of the
1st century BC, the Romans were
in control. The Second Temple
period ended in AD 70 with,
yet again, the destruction of
the Temple and Jerusalem, this
time by the Romans. When the
emperor Constantine converted
to Christianity early in the 4th
century, Jerusalem became a
Christian city. Jerusalem finally
succumbed to the Muslim

invaders in AD 640 and the
Islamic Dome of the Rock was
built in AD 691 on the site of the
Temple.

The Turks were ascendant
until the arrival of the Crusaders
at the end of the 11th century, but
although they captured the entire
country, they never completely
removed the Muslim threat,
and in 1517 Jerusalem and all
of Palestine became part of the
greater Ottoman Empire. The
Turks ruled for 400 years, during
which time they constructed the
present walls of the Old City.

By the close of World War
I the Ottoman Empire had
crumbled and the British army
entered Jerusalem in 1917. The
British received a mandate from
the League of Nations to rule
Palestine, and they remained here
until 1948 when Israel's War of
Independence erupted. The State
of Israel was born, but Jerusalem
became a divided city: the western
part remained in Israeli hands

Above: *The Dome of the Rock dominates the old city of Jerusalem*

Above: *Mount Scopus overlooks the Old City*

but the eastern half, including the Old City, fell to the Jordanians. For nineteen years the city lived with a concrete wall down its centre, marking the international border between Jordan and Israel. In 1967 during the Six Day War, Israel recaptured east Jerusalem from the Jordanians and reunited the city.

For a timeline of the main battles for Jerusalem see page 118.

Above: *There is a vast Jewish cemetery on the Mount of Olives*

Mount Scopus

Mount Scopus belongs to the same ridge as the Mount of Olives. *Skopos* is Greek for 'watch'—this has always been an important vantage point to the east and south, and a strategic military target.

Both the Hebrew University, established in 1918, and the Hadassah hospital established in 1934, flourished here until 1948. When the War of Independence ended, Mount Scopus remained in Israeli hands, but the territory surrounding it fell to the Jordanians. As regular traffic could not be maintained up and down the hill, both the university and the hospital were forced to establish new premises in the western part of the city. Once the area around Mount Scopus was freed during the Six Day War of 1967, both institutions decided to return to their original homes. As a result, today there are two Hadassah hospitals in Jerusalem and the Hebrew University has two campuses.

The Church of the Ascension

This small dome-shaped building on the western side of the Mount of Olives is supposedly built on the site where Jesus ascended into heaven (Luke 24:50–53; Acts 1:4–11). On the floor inside the building the tourist will be shown a mark, which is said to be the footprint of Christ. There is no historical evidence for this, and the tradition only dates back to the Crusader period. It is important to note that Muslims regard Jesus as a Prophet but not as the Son of God; they do not accept the crucifixion or the resurrection, but they do accept the ascension. For this reason, they allow various Christian denominations to celebrate the Feast of the Ascension at the church once a year.

The history of this church is typical of most churches in Israel. It was built in the 4th century AD when Byzantine monks came looking for places mentioned in the Scriptures. On these sites they built dozens of churches, almost all of which were destroyed during the Persian invasion of 614. The Crusaders rebuilt the churches during the 12th century, but when they were defeated by the Muslims less than a hundred years later, the churches were either destroyed or converted into mosques or for other purposes. Islam reveres the prophets of Judaism and Christianity and accepts many of their historic sites as their own.

The original Byzantine building of the Church of the Ascension had two concentric circles of pillars surrounding the stone to which local tradition attributes the ascension of Jesus. When the Crusaders rebuilt the church they left the site of the ascension open to the air, and surrounded it with arches supported by columns. The spot was subsequently walled in and roofed when the Muslims

Above: *Jews believe that when Messiah comes those buried on the Mount of Olives will rise first*

Above: *The traditional route of the Palm Sunday road leads down the Mount of Olives*

Above: *Jesus wept on the Mount of Olives as he looked over Jerusalem and spoke of her future destruction*

converted the church into a mosque; the minaret and prayer room are just on the other side of the entrance wall.

The Church of the Pater Noster (Eleona)

Also known as Eleona Basilica (Greek 'Olive Tree'), this church was first built in AD 333 by Queen Helena, the very devout mother of the emperor Constantine. It marks the traditional place where Jesus is thought to have taught the disciples to pray on the Mount of Olives (Luke 11:1–4). The Lord's Prayer is displayed here in over sixty different languages.

The Palm Sunday Walk

This walk follows the last part of the Palm Sunday route from Bethphage (a little village on the eastern slope) into the Old City of Jerusalem (Mark 11:1–11). In Bible times, Bethphage was regarded as being just within the boundary of Jerusalem. The walk begins from the top of the Mount of Olives, descending past the Jewish cemetery, an ancient and important burial ground still in use today for those who can afford it. According to Jewish tradition when the Messiah arrives he will pass over the Mount of Olives on his way up to the Temple Mount. Jews believe that whoever is buried here will be among the first to be resurrected when the Messiah comes.

The Church of Dominus Flevit

This church commemorates the occasion on the Mount of Olives when Jesus looked out on the city of Jerusalem and wept (*Dominus Flevit* means 'the Lord wept') over its imminent destruction (Luke 19:41–44)). The building was designed by a Franciscan architect named Antonio Barluzzi who was noted for incorporating the theme of a holy site into his work.

Thus the church is tear-shaped and looks west towards Jerusalem just as Jesus would have done—notwithstanding the tradition of churches facing east

Not far from Dominus Flevit is an ancient tomb. Although Jews worldwide today bury their dead in the ground, in ancient times they used tombs like this one. The tombs were caves hewn out of the natural rock in burial areas outside the boundaries of the city. They usually had several rooms, among them a chamber with stone shelves carved into the rock. The body was anointed with oil and wrapped in a plain white funeral shroud according to Jewish custom. It was then laid to rest on one of the stone shelves and the tomb was sealed,

Above: The Garden of Gethsemane still evokes thoughts of the night before Jesus was crucified

usually with a large rolling stone. When the flesh had decomposed and only the bones were left, the family members returned to the tomb and placed the bones in a stone box called an 'ossuary' which was stored in another part of the tomb. The tomb belonging to Joseph of Arimathea, where Jesus' body was laid to rest, was probably very similar to this one.

The Basilica of the Agony

The Basilica of the Agony (or Church of All Nations) commemorates the occasion in the Garden when the soldiers arrested Jesus. The church windows are of glass, but stained deep purple to keep the sanctuary dark, just as it was on the night of the arrest. The mosaics on the ceiling are a star-studded sky, and the scenes on the front wall of the church show the arrival of Judas Iscariot and the soldiers in the garden.

Above: The Golden Gate, or Gate Beautiful, is currently blocked up; however, Jews believe it will be reopened for the Messiah to pass through when he walks into Jerusalem from the Mount of Olives

Olives on the east. Due to the accumulation of debris over the centuries, the bed of the valley is reckoned to be 2·5m to 15m (10 to 50ft) higher than it would have been when Jesus walked here. The Judean kings owned property in the Valley, and hence it became known as the Kings' Valley. David crossed the valley when fleeing from Absalom (2 Samuel 15:23). In fact, Absalom set up a monument for himself in the Kings' Valley (2 Samuel 18:18).

Above: The darkness inside the Basilica of the Agony was designed to commemorate the night that Jesus prayed in Gethsemane

The Kidron Valley

The Kidron Valley is three miles long, separating Jerusalem on the west, from the Mount of

St Peter in Gallicantu

According to tradition, this was the site of the palace of high priest Caiaphas, where Jesus was brought to prison after his arrest. Its name (Gallicantu means 'cock's crow)' commemorates the story of Peter's triple denial of Christ and the cock crowing twice

The Garden of Gethsemane

Gethsemane was just across the Kidron Valley (John 18:1). Here Jesus prayed 'Father, if it is your will, take this cup away from me; nevertheless not my will but yours, be done' (Luke 22:42). His agony was intense, so that his sweat was like great drops of blood. Returning to his disciples, he found them asleep (Matthew 26:42–46). Judas came, leading a crowd of officials, and identified Jesus with a kiss. They arrested him, and led him away. Even

his closest disciples left him and fled (Matthew 26:47–56).

Today, many varieties of flowers bloom the year round in the garden, though during Jesus' time it was probably more of a commercial garden producing olive oil, an important local commodity. The name 'Gethsemane' (Matthew 26:36) comes from the Hebrew words gat (press) and shmanim (oils), indicating that there was probably an olive press here used to extract oil from the fruit of the trees in the garden. In this place where olives

were crushed, Jesus experienced new depths of sorrows (Luke 22:44).

Although the olive trees in the garden are very old—some go back to the Byzantine period—they are not the same trees that Jesus would have walked amongst; the 1st century Jewish historian Josephus records that the Romans burned everything to ashes in Jerusalem in the year AD 70. However, olive trees are often born from the roots of dead ones, so that these trees are probably the direct descendants of the trees from Jesus' day.

(Mark 14). In the courtyard of the church is a statue that describes the events of the denial of Jesus by Peter, the cock (seen on the top), the maid, and the Roman soldier; the inscription is part of Luke 22:57.

In the basement of the church is a cave that resembles a bottle dungeon. According to tradition Jesus was held at this place after his arrest. Copies of Psalm 88 are here in many languages, for it speaks of one who is unjustly imprisoned in darkness for crimes he did not commit. Above the cell has been identified the 'Place of Scourging'. Two holes in a lintel, with raised places for the feet carved out of the stone, may mark the spot where a victim was tied up before being whipped. On the north side of the Church is an ancient staircase that is perhaps the way that Jesus was led from his arrest in the Garden of Gethsemane.

The Church of St Anne

According to tradition, this church is believed to have been the home of Anne, the mother of Mary. The building, almost perfectly intact, is one of the finest examples of Crusader architecture in Israel. After the Crusaders were defeated by the Muslims in 1187 it was converted to a school and preserved beautifully for centuries. A five-line Arabic inscription still remains over the main door. However, the church was damaged by an Israeli shell which fell accidentally on the Old City during the Six Day War in 1967. The roof was repaired so expertly, however, that it is virtually impossible to detect where the damage occurred.

It is interesting to note that this site was offered to Queen Victoria. The offer was declined, but if she had accepted it, St Anne's could well have become

Above: *There is a spectacular view of Jerusalem through the window of the Dominus Flevit Chapel*

Left: The Kidron Valley separates Jerusalem from the Mount of Olives

Below: A plaque reminds visitors of the sufferings of Jesus in Gethsemane

the Anglican Cathedral in Jerusalem. The Church of St Anne is probably best known for its outstanding acoustics; it is an excellent place to sing, and even a handful of people sound like a large choir.

The Bethesda Pools

The Bethesda Pools are referred to in the Bible as the location of Jesus' healing of the paralytic. The description of the place in John 5:1–15 is very specific: It was near the Sheep Gate, was called Bethesda, and had five porches. In 1888 a place was unearthed that perfectly matched this description, just north of the Temple Mount, close to the Sheep Gate (Lions' Gate or St Stephen's Gate). The Pool of Bethesda consisted of two rectangular pools, separated by a stone partition twenty feet thick, on which the 5th porch once stood.

According to John 5:10 the Jews were angry when the healed man picked up his bed and walked away with it on the Sabbath. In Judaism, work is defined very broadly to include a number of activities which are forbidden on the Sabbath according to Jewish law, including carrying burdens. Therefore, when the healed man picked up his mat and walked away with it, the crowd of observant Jews was very angry.

The Bethesda Pools served as reservoirs to supply the temple with large quantities of water during the Hasmonean era (140–37 B.C.). The Hasmonean Kingdom was an autonomous Jewish State, established under the leadership of Judas Maccabaeus in 140 B.C.

The Stone Pavement (Lithostratos)

The Sisters of Zion Convent houses three items of interest: the Struthion Pool was part of the moat of the Antonia Fortress and

Above: St Peter in Gallicantu recalls Peter's denial of Jesus

Above: A monument at St Peter in Gallicantu shows the cockerel and the girl with Peter and the soldiers

lay open to the air during Jesus' time here. On the Pavement, or Gabbatha (John 19:13), games carved into the stone were for many years believed to have been the work of the Roman soldiers who were guarding Jesus. The Ecce Homo Arch, over the same place, was thought to be where Jesus stood when Pilate came out and declared: 'Behold the Man' (John 19:5). It is now known that the roof over the pool and the arch were constructed about 100 years after the death of Jesus. When the Romans rebuilt Jerusalem in AD 132 the Emperor Hadrian constructed a central marketplace over the pool; he built a roof to cover the pool and serve as the floor of the market. Hadrian also built a triple victory arch in the centre of the marketplace, traditionally known as the Ecce Homo Arch. Hence the arch and the games etched in the stones were

from a period about one hundred years after the time of Jesus.

Via Dolorosa—The Way of the Cross

Although there is no evidence that this is the route Jesus took to the cross, many visitors find it useful to follow the Via Dolorosa, or way of suffering, as a way of focussing their minds on the passion of Christ.

The Church of the Holy Sepulchre

This church is considered by some to be the site of the burial and resurrection of Jesus Christ. In the 4th century, Helena, the mother of Emperor Constantine and, like her son, a convert to Christianity, travelled to Palestine and identified the location of the crucifixion; the emperor then built a magnificent church. The church was destroyed and rebuilt several times over the

Above: *The Pools of Bethesda are within the compound of the Church of St Anne near the Lions Gate*

Above: *The Stone Pavement in the Sisters of Zion Convent shows the markings of Roman games*

centuries. The building standing today dates from the 12th century.

Control of the Church of the Holy Sepulchre is zealously guarded by different denominations. The Greek Orthodox, Roman Catholics, Armenians and Copts are among those that oversee different parts of the Church. In the 12th century, fighting among different denominations over who should keep the key to the church led the Arab conqueror Saladin to entrust the key to the Muslim Nuseibeh and Joudeh families. Today, eight centuries later, the 10–inch metal key is still safeguarded in the house of the Joudeh family. In 1840 a devastating fire caused a panic that led to many deaths, and agreement was finally reached in June 1999 to open another exit; but this has provoked a new dispute over who will have the key to the new door!

The Temple Church in London was built by the Knights Templar, the order of crusading monks founded to protect pilgrims on their way to and from Jerusalem in the 12th century. It was designed to recall the holiest place in the Crusaders' world: the Church of the Holy Sepulchre in Jerusalem.

Centre: *The Via Dolorosa, or Way of Sorrows, leads into the Old City*

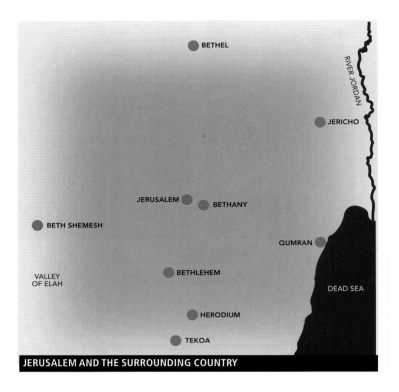

BETHEL

RIVER JORDAN

JERICHO

JERUSALEM   BETHANY

BETH SHEMESH

QUMRAN

VALLEY
OF ELAH

BETHLEHEM

DEAD SEA

HERODIUM

TEKOA

JERUSALEM AND THE SURROUNDING COUNTRY

TRAVEL INFORMATION

Unless otherwise noted most places in this travel section will be found on the websites: http://www.science.co.il/nature.asp OR www.sacred-destinations.com

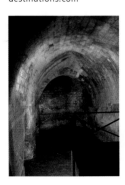

Bethesda Pools

The Bethesda Pools are at St Anne's Church, the Lions' Gate, Old City.

Open from Mon–Sat 8am–noon and 2–5pm (until 6pm in summer); closed Sunday

The Sisters of Zion Convent includes the Roman Pavement (or Lithostratos) and Herod's Cistern—see the website: www.eccehomoconvent.com

The Church of the Holy Sepulchre

Suq Khan e-Zeit and Christian Quarter Rd., Jerusalem, Israel
☎ 02/627–3314

Open: Apr.–Sept., daily 5am–8pm; Oct.–Mar., daily 5 AM–7 PM.

Dress code: No shorts or sleeveless shirts.

Christ Church

Website: www.cmj.org.uk
Christ Church, P.O.B. 14037, Jaffa Gate, Old City, Jerusalem
☎ (0)2 627 7727
Christ Church was the first Protestant church to be established in the Middle East. Situated just inside the Jaffa

Right: The Ecce Homo Arch is the traditional site where Pilate brought out Jesus with the words 'Behold, the man' (Ecce homo)

Above: Many believe that Jesus was buried on the site of the Church of the Holy Sepulchre

Left: For visitors, Herod's water cistern is a welcome relief from the heat outside

Gate of the Old City of Jerusalem, it was built in the style of a synagogue. Consecrated in 1849 as an Anglican Church, it is now home to several congregations. There are international English-speaking congregation (Anglican) services on Sundays and a Hebrew-speaking congregation meeting on Saturdays. Romanian and Filipino congregations also worship here.

The Sunday morning English service is at 0930.

For shopping, there is an excellent Christian bookshop next to Christchurch, with many other gift ideas too.

⑦ Jerusalem the Golden

Jerusalem is one of the most ancient cities in the world. However, for Christians, Jews and Muslims, which is half the human race, it occupies a special place as the 'Holy City'

The Old City of Jerusalem covers nearly one square kilometre (250 acres). The surrounding walls date to the rule of the Ottoman Sultan, Suleiman the Magnificent (1520–1566). Work began on them in 1537 and was not completed until 1541.

The Old City is divided into four quarters, which are each named after the respective ethnic grouping. The divisions run north to south from Damascus Gate to Zion Gate, and east to west from the Lions' Gate to Jaffa Gate (See The Cardo on page 94).

The Christian Quarter. Entering the Old City through the Jaffa Gate and walking along David Street, the Christian Quarter is on the left. The buildings that dominate this quarter include mostly churches, chapels, monasteries, schools, missions and hospices. The best shopping within the Christian quarter is to be found along David Street and the small alleyways adjoining.

The Muslim Quarter. The Lions' Gate leads into the Muslim Quarter, which contains some significant sites of interest including the most famous street in the old city, the Via Dolorosa. Not far from Lions' Gate on St Mary's Street is the

Facing page: An aerial view of Jerusalem shows the Western Wall and the Temple Mount area

Above: The Dome is overlaid with gold and was paid for by King Hussein of Jordan

Church of St Anne. Close by is the excavated site of the Pools of Bethesda (see page 85). The Via Dolorosa leads into the Old City, passing groups of men smoking water pipes, shops catering for tourists, and stalls selling Arab pastries, Turkish coffee, fruit and vegetables, brass ornaments, and olive wood gifts. The sights and smells are an essential part of the itinerary for every visitor.

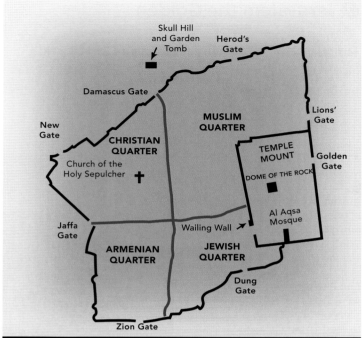

MAP SHOWING THE GATES AND FOUR QUARTERS OF OLD JERUSALEM

The Armenian Quarter.
This is located in the south-west section of the Old City. It is entered either through the Jaffa Gate or Zion Gate. This is a world on its own, where priests and bishops may be heard speaking in Aramaic. This section of the Christian church has maintained its own language, customs and calendar since separating from the western

church in AD 491. One of the best known buildings in the Armenian Quarter is St Mark's House, just off St James Street. This is the See of the Syrian Archbishop of Jerusalem, and a Syrian Orthodox Monastery dating back to the 12th century. The Armenians believe that this is the house of Mary, the mother of Mark, where Peter went after being delivered from

Above: In the Muslim Quarter of the Old City there is a Souk or Bazaar

Above: Walking on the ramparts provides superb views over Jerusalem

established his city on the slopes just south of the Temple Mount, known as the Ophel. As the population grew, the overflow settled in the area of the present Jewish Quarter. Archaeologists have found Jewish settlements here dating back to the 7th and 8th centuries BC. This became known as the Upper City, to distinguish it from the original Lower City.

The Broad Wall

Built by Hezekiah in 701 BC, together with Hezekiah's Tunnel it formed Jerusalem's defence system against the invading Assyrians. At that time the Israelite nation was divided: the ten tribes of Israel occupied the north (Israel), and Judah and Benjamin were in the south (Judah). In 722 BC the Assyrians had defeated the north and either killed, enslaved or deported most of its population. Hezekiah built a second defensive wall

prison (Acts 12:12). Their belief is that this is the site of the Upper Room, and also where Peter founded the first Church.

The Jewish Quarter. The Dung Gate leads into the Jewish Quarter, which is on the western side of the Western Wall. David

Above: Men and Women have their separate sections at the Western or Wailing Wall

Right: The Medba Map was created in the time of the emperor Justinian in the 6th century AD and was discovered on the floor of a church in the village of Madaba in Jordan

(2 Chronicles 32:5) and cut off the water supply from Jerusalem to deny it to the Assyrians (vs 3–4). See Hezekiah's Tunnel on page 103 and Lachish on page 70. 2 Chronicles 32:20–21 records that the Assyrian army was decimated overnight by the hand of God.

The Burnt House

This is a museum in the Jewish Quarter, with a multimedia presentation. It gives a fascinating insight into 1st century life. The museum building acquired its name because its remains were discovered under a layer of ashes. It was destroyed by fire a month after the Second Temple was destroyed by the Romans in AD 70. It had been owned by the Katroses, a family of priests, who may have prepared incense for the temple here.

The Cardo

The 'Cardo Maximus' (or simply 'Cardo'—Latin for 'hinge') was the main street of Roman-Byzantine Jerusalem. Running north to south from the Damascus Gate, it cut the city in half. It was intersected by the other major

thoroughfare, the 'Decumanus' which ran west to east from the Jaffa Gate. These two main roads quartered ancient Jerusalem into what are now the Christian, Muslim, Jewish and Armenian quarters. The Cardo was a very broad street lined on either side by huge pillars which supported red-tiled roofs. This street served as the main marketplace of the city. Some of the original paving stones can still be seen, and a section of the street later covered with vaulted arches by the Crusaders is still intact. Today the recreated Cardo serves as the commercial centre of the Jewish Quarter, although the shops cater

Above: The Burnt House dates back to the 1st century AD and provides a good insight into life then

Jerusalem's walls

The cry of Nehemiah during Israel's captivity was 'The wall of Jerusalem is also broken down, and its gates are burned with fire' (Nehemiah 1:3). During its long history of conflict, Jerusalem has been attacked many times and its walls destroyed at least five times. The present walls have resulted from various periods of construction. Their lines mostly follow the Crusader walls of 1099, but partly also the walls surrounding Hadrian's 2nd century Roman colony Aelia Capitolina. The walls themselves are impressively large, averaging 12m (40ft) high, with eight gates and 34 towers. Measuring about 4km (2·5mi) around, the more adventurous are easily able to walk on the ramparts. For a small fee, they provide a superb view of the city that would be impossible to see otherwise. The visitor is able to access the path along the walls from Jaffa, Damascus, Lions' or Zion's Gates, although it is not possible to walk around the entire city. It is not permitted to walk along the wall surrounding the Temple Mount. It is recommended to walk from Jaffa Gate to the Dung Gate.

for tourists rather than local residents.

Further along the Cardo is a reproduction of the Medba Map, a 6th century Byzantine mosaic of the Holy Land found on the floor of a church in Jordan. Much of the original map was destroyed but the part showing Jerusalem is in excellent condition and is the oldest known map of the city. Although slightly inaccurate, the map very clearly shows the Cardo leading from Damascus Gate south and lined by pillars, as well as the Cardo Valensis, another main market street leading down towards the Temple Mount. Most of the buildings pictured on the map are churches, the most prominent one being the Church of the Holy Sepulchre. The Nea Church, also visible, was built by the emperor Justinian and is said to have been the largest and most beautiful church in Jerusalem. The Temple Mount is noticeably absent, having been destroyed by the Romans in AD 70.

From the Jaffa Gate side of the city, the most striking landmark is the Citadel, which is marked by David's Tower, a misnomer

Above: *A walk through the Old City*

Right: The Damascus Gate leads through the Muslim Quarter to the Western Wall

given that the cylindrical structure dates from the 16th century. By contrast, the tall, square tower is 2,000 years old and was built by Herod.

The gates of the city (see map on page 92)

From the walls one gains a birds-eye view of the eight city gates. If we think of the old city as the face of a clock, the main gate of Jerusalem is the **Damascus Gate** at 12 noon. The road from Jerusalem to Damascus begins here, and passes through Shechem. Sometimes it is called the Shechem Gate. Underneath the Damascus Gate, the gate from the time of Hadrian's conquest of Jerusalem still bears a Roman inscription. It was the main thoroughfare at the time of the Roman Empire.

At one o'clock on a map of the Old City is **Herod's Gate.** The name comes from a medieval tradition that wrongly assumed Herod Antipas had lived in a palace nearby. In reality, his residence was on Mount Zion.

The **Lions' Gate (or Sheep Gate)** is at 2 o'clock, named after the two lions which are carved on either side of the entrance. They are emblems of the Mameluke Sultan, Baybars. Walking up from the Kidron Valley, this gate leads to the Via Dolorosa. It is also known as St Stephen's Gate because a tradition says that Stephen, the first Christian martyr walked out through this gate before he was stoned to death (Acts 7:54–60). On 7 June 1967 Israel's army fought its way through the Lions' Gate; bullet marks can still be seen on the walls of this gate.

At 3 o'clock we come to the **Golden Gate**, the only gate that is closed. Also known as the Eastern Gate, it is the oldest and best known of all. It is thought to have been built in the 5th century by Eudocia, the wife of the Byzantine Emperor King Theodosius II. This has two arches, the northern arch being called 'The Gate of Repentance' and the southern arch 'The Gate of Mercy'. It was the main entrance to Jerusalem in both the Old and New Testaments and it leads out to the Kidron Valley and the Mount of Olives. Jews believe that one day the Messiah will walk from the Mount of Olives to the Temple Mount through this gate. Jesus made his triumphal entry into Jerusalem through this gate (Matthew 21:8–11); and he also left the city here to pray in the Garden of Gethsemane (Matthew 26:30, 36). No visit to Jerusalem is complete without a photo of the Golden Gate from the Mount of Olives.

The **Dung Gate** is at 4 o'clock. The Crusaders knew it as the Tanner's Gate. However, from the time of Nehemiah, it has been called the Dung Gate (Nehemiah 2:13). This is because refuse was taken through this gate to burn in the Hinnom Valley below. Jesus used this image when he spoke of Gehenna (Hinnom) as the place where the worm does not die and the fire is not quenched (Mark 9:42–50).

Above: *The Golden Gate is best seen from the Temple Mount*

The **Zion Gate** is at 6 o'clock and the local Arab population call it the Gate of David because it is close to the supposed site of David's tomb (for which there is little evidence). For this reason, Muslims treat this gate with respect. The tomb is draped with a heavy blue cloth, and visitors should respect the fact that for some Jews this is a place of prayer. Therefore women must be appropriately dressed, and men must wear a skull cap in order to enter. It is housed within the same complex of buildings that includes the site of the Upper Room.

The **Jaffa Gate,** at 9 o'clock, is the busiest. The road to Bethlehem and Hebron runs from here, as does the road to Jaffa and the Mediterranean.

The final gate is the **New Gate** at 10 o'clock. Built in 1887 by Sultan Abdul Hamid, it became known as the Sultan's Gate, and it provides entry into the Christian Quarter.

Above: Many Jewish men wear a prayer shawl or Tallit when they pray

The Western Wall

Herod the Great enlarged the courtyard surrounding the Temple where all the visitors gathered for the three pilgrimage festivals: Pesach (Passover), Shavuot (Pentecost) and Sukkot (Tabernacles). He did this by extending the Temple Mount platform using four retaining walls. Only the western wall of the extended platform now remains. It is often wrongly thought to be the western wall of the Temple, but the Temple was on top of the platform and was completely destroyed by the Romans in AD 70. The Western Wall is also known as the Wailing Wall because Jews come here to pray and bemoan the destruction of the Temple. The Wall has the status of a synagogue, hence the partition down the middle; in traditional Jewish synagogues men and women sit separately during prayers. Jews often write out prayers on small notes and wedge them between the stones

of the Wall, believing that the holiness of this site assures them of answers. On Saturdays, Mondays and Thursdays, Bar Mitzvahs are usually celebrated here. The Bar Mitzvah is the Jewish coming-of-age ceremony, when a boy is initiated into adulthood by being called up to read from the Torah (first five books of the Old Testament) for the first time.

The Temple Mount

At the entrance to the Temple Mount is a sign warning all Jews that they are forbidden to enter the area, owing to its sanctity. The Temple of Solomon was built to house the Ark of the Covenant which was kept in the Holy of Holies, the innermost room of the Temple which was so sacred that only the High Priest was permitted to enter it and only once a year—on Yom Kippur, the Day of Atonement. The Ark disappeared sometime during the First Temple period

---

The Temple Mount—a sacrifice provided

Christians, Jews and Muslims are all interested in the Temple Mount because it is built on the site of Mount Moriah. Abraham was told by God to take his 'only son' Isaac to the top of Mount Moriah and sacrifice him to the LORD (Genesis 22:1–14). Abraham learned that the LORD would provide his own sacrifice there. Much later, it became the threshing floor of Araunah, which David purchased as a place of sacrifice, to take away God's judgement from the people (2 Samuel 24:15–25). David built there an altar to the LORD, and offered burnt offerings and peace offerings. He also gathered the materials for the Temple, which his son Solomon built on this site (1 Chronicles 22:5). The temple was destroyed by Nebuchadnezzar in 586 BC, rebuilt and then destroyed again by the Romans in AD 70. Muslims made Mount Moriah a shrine when they captured Jerusalem in AD 639.

---

and today the Temple itself is gone. But in the minds of strict Jews, the Holy of Holies is as sacred as when the Temple existed, and they believe that by entering the Temple Mount they risk walking through the Holy of Holies; however, non-religious Jews do enter the Temple Mount.

Despite the existence of two Muslim shrines on this holy Jewish site, Jewish tradition claims that the Temple will be rebuilt when the Messiah arrives; they wait patiently. Today the Temple Mount is the third holiest site for Islam, after Mecca and Medina in Saudi Arabia. The Dome of the Rock was built in AD 691 and the El Aksa Mosque was constructed in the early 8th century to provide room for many worshippers on the Temple Mount. It is the largest and most important mosque in Israel.

Hezekiah's Tunnel

The village of Silwan (or Siloam) is just beyond the southeast corner of the Old City walls. As the Silwan Road enters the village, there is an entrance to the Gihon Spring, one of Jerusalem's earliest water sources. The Jebusites first dug an underground water shaft through to this natural spring some three thousand years ago. It was this shaft that David's men used in order to enter and capture Jerusalem (2 Samuel 5:6–10). As a result of this military triumph, Jerusalem became the

Above: The ramparts walk can be accessed near Jaffa gate

'City of David,' and therefore also his spiritual and his political headquarters. The Gihon Spring later became the location for Solomon's coronation as Israel's third king (1 Kings 1:33–45).

Being outside the city wall, the Gihon Spring was also open to Israel's enemies, leaving them vulnerable. When Sennacherib of Assyria invaded the land and threatened Jerusalem in 701 BC (2 Kings 18:17–21), in order to secure their water source, King Hezekiah had a tunnel carved out of the rock in the hill Ophel, on the south side of Mount Moriah. He also had a reservoir built at the end of the tunnel, within the walls of the lower city, called the Pool of Siloam. The tunnel was constructed by working from both ends simultaneously, probably along the course of a natural cleft in the rock. An inscription in the rock at the end of the tunnel describes the completion of the project. It zig-zags for 540m (1770ft), but if it had followed a straight line the length would have been 335m (1070 ft). The construction is described in (2 Kings 20:20 and 2 Chronicles 32:30).

Siloam Inscription

The inscription in Hezekiah's Tunnel was discovered in 1880 by a boy who was bathing in the waters of the Gihon Spring, and it was studied by Conrad Schick, one of the first explorers of Jerusalem. Engraved in the rock, the inscription describes the meeting of the two groups of hewers who had begun digging from opposite ends of the tunnel: 'The tunnelling was completed … While the hewers wielded the axe, each man toward his fellow … there was heard a man's voice calling to his fellow … the

Above: The Temple Mount is quiet these days and closely protected by Islamic authorities

Above: The Citadel is next to David's Tower by the Jaffa Gate

hewers hacked each toward the other, axe against axe, and the water flowed from the spring to the pool, a distance of 1,200 cubits ...' The inscription is now in the Istanbul Museum.

Pools of Siloam

In 2005 archaeologists working in the City of David uncovered the edge of what they believe is the Pool of Siloam from the time of Jesus (John 9). These excavations are located on the west side of the City of David. Previously a pool at one end of Hezekiah's Tunnel was thought to be the correct site. There are clear remains around this pool from the Byzantine church built by Empress Eudocia, who had married the Emperor Theodosius II and became a Christian in AD 421. Excavations continue to reveal more sections of the pool on the northern and southern ends. Several shafts at the northern end of the pool have revealed large paving stones. On the southern end, excavations have uncovered a large wall and a section of the pool from the Old Testament period.

The Herodian Road

This short piece of road, dating back to the time of David, was discovered by archaeologists at the end of the 19th century. In 1963 Dame Kathleen Kenyon unearthed a further portion of this road.

Right:
Hezekiah's Tunnel is further archaeological evidence of the reliability of the Bible

Left: *A section of Nehemiah's Broad Wall can see seen near the Cardo*

Below left: *Research is currently taking place on what is believed to be the original Pools of Siloam*

TRAVEL INFORMATION

Unless otherwise noted most places in this travel section will be found on the websites: http://www.science.co.il/nature.asp OR www.sacred-destinations.com

Ramparts Walk

Access to the ramparts is on either side of the Jaffa Gate. One direction runs just over one mile up from Jaffa Gate and along the north wall and nearly half way down the east side to the edge of the Temple Mount. The other direction goes down from Jaffa Gate and along most of the south wall. The only

area to which access is denied for political and security reasons is that which borders the Temple Mount and Western Wall.

The Western Wall Tunnels

See http://www.aish.com/seminars/tunneltours/ To schedule a tour, ✆ 972–2–6271333

A tour of the Western Wall Tunnels is a fascinating journey through time. The archaeology of the site brings to life the history of Jerusalem. Tours of the tunnels are taken only with guides and must be scheduled in advance. Tours are available for individuals and groups, and they take about an hour and a quarter in total. The tour is suitable for the general public, for groups of up to 30.

The Western Wall Tunnels are open to visitors Sunday to Thursday, from 0800 to evening (depending on

scheduled visits). On Fridays and the eve of holidays, the site is open from 0800 to 1230.

The site is closed on the Sabbath and Jewish holidays, the eve of Yom Kippur, Independence Day, and Tisha Be'Av. On the Intermediate days of Passover and Succot (Tabernacles), the Western Wall Tunnels will be open as usual (for a fee and by advanced reservation).

The Burnt House

The entrance to the house is marked on a modern door in the Seven Arches off Misgav Ladach Road (ask if you have difficulty finding the door). The house is open Sunday to Thursday from 0900 to 1700, on Friday from 0900 until 1200. There is a 12–minute slide presentation that explains its history, and provides background information on the Herodian Quarter as well. The English soundtrack normally runs

George Bill

orazy.co.uk/qa

S

Above: David's Tower is one of the oldest structures in the Old City

Below right: The traditional site of the Pool of Siloam is at the end of Hezekiah's Tunnel

way forks from Jericho Road.

Open: Sunday to Thursday 0900–1700, Friday until 1500

Where to shop

There is an excellent shop in the Jewish Quarter of the Old City, near the Cardo, called Shorashim. It has become a favourite place for visitors looking for a special gift, or for those that just want a welcoming place to browse and chat with the owners. They sell a wide variety of items for those with an interest in Judaica. But they are happy to talk and explain the significance of these things too. If you cannot visit, they also sell on-line at http://www.shorashim.net/

at 0930 and 1130 and 1330 and 1530.

The Davidson Centre

Website: www.archpark.org.il
The Davidson Centre is the Jerusalem Archaeological Park which includes the Temple Mount excavations near the Dung Gate.

Open: Sunday to Thursday 0800–1700; Friday 0800–1400; Closed on Saturdays and Jewish holidays

Hezekiah's Tunnel

The tunnel is one-third of a mile long, and takes about 30 minutes to walk through. Good waterproof footwear is required, and possibly a change of clothes as one is walking through water up to 1m (3·3ft) deep. A good torch is essential, ideally a head torch that leaves one's hands free. Please be aware that the tunnel gets very narrow at certain points. The approach to the spring from the Silwan

⑧ Outside a city wall

'My eyes have seen your salvation
Which you have prepared before the face of all peoples,
A light to bring revelation to the Gentiles,
And the glory of your people Israel'
Luke 2:30–32

Driving into Jerusalem today, it is hard to imagine that prior to 1948 there were hardly any houses outside the city walls. Almost all the buildings we now see have been constructed since the six day war of 1967. On the Judaean hills around the city, shepherds once tended their sheep. On those same hills the visitor will now see the Israeli Parliament buildings, an enviable University, and the National Israel Museum. The city boundaries have been further extended by tall hotels and new housing developments that edge their way into desert. This is modern Jerusalem.

Facing page: The Garden Tomb is next to Gordon's Calvary and is thought by some to be in the garden of Joseph of Arimathea where Jesus was buried

Above: The British Government gave the Menorah as a gift to Israel following the establishment of the State of Israel

The Menorah
On the Titus Arch in Rome, celebrating the Emperor's victory over the Jewish rebellion, is the only known depiction of the great Menorah, the seven-branched candlestick from the Second (Herod's) Temple. This has come to symbolise the State of Israel. Opposite the entrance to the Israeli Parliament building, the *Knesset*, stands a large Menorah, 5m (16ft) high and 4m (13ft) wide. It was sculptured by Beno Elkan, with 29 different scenes from Jewish history.

Above: The Israeli Parliament is called the Knesset

The Knesset

The Knesset, Israel's House of Parliament, was dedicated in 1966. The name 'Knesset' derives from the great assembly which convened in Jerusalem after the return of the Jews to Israel from exile in Babylon, in the 5th century BC. Inside the building are many works by the artist Marc Chagall, including wall and floor mosaics and the triple tapestries entitled The Creation, Exodus and Entry in Jerusalem.

The Shrine of the Book

This building is shaped like the lids of the earthenware jars in which the Dead Sea Scrolls were found. Some of the scrolls were written on papyrus (a thick paper-like material which is made from the pith of the papyrus plant), while many of them were written on animal hide. Due to the fragility of the scrolls, they are displayed on a rotation system. The museum also holds other rare manuscripts.

Scale Model of Jerusalem

Hans Broch, the owner of the Holy Land Hotel, paid for a scale model of Jerusalem at the time of the Second Temple to be constructed in the hotel grounds. It was begun in 1965 and completed in 1968, with adjustments being made as archaeological work progresses in the ancient city. It is 1:50 in scale and gives an idea of Jerusalem during the life of Jesus.

Above: The Shrine of the Book houses the Dead Sea Scrolls and is shaped like the lid of the stone jars in which they were discovered

Yad Vashem—The Holocaust History Museum

Newly built in 2005, the Holocaust History Museum uses over 2,500 genuine artefacts, collected over the last fifty years, including testimonies, photographs, film clips, art and music. The original voices of more than ninety individuals movingly tell the story of the Holocaust. The Museum is

on the site include The Hall of Remembrance, a solemn tent-like structure with the names of the six death camps marked out on the floor. In front of the memorial flame, a crypt contains the ashes of victims.

The Children's Memorial is a moving tribute to approximately one and a half million Jewish children who died in the Holocaust. The Avenue of the

Left: At the same site as the Israel Museum there is an excellent scale model of Jerusalem at the time of the Second Temple. This provides a useful overview of the Old City

purposely built like a prism into a hillside, with both ends jutting into the open air. The central story runs from one end to the other, and the various 'chapters' branch out on either side, telling in chronological order the history of the Holocaust—a turning point for the Jewish nation and for the world. Visitors descend into the mountain, and then ascend gently towards the end, with a spectacular view of Jerusalem. A full tour of the entire Museum takes two to three hours, and most visitors need to carefully choose which 'chapters' to spend their time in. In addition to the main Museum, other buildings

Righteous among the Nations honours the non-Jews who risked their lives to help Jews during the Holocaust. Two thousand trees, representing new life, have been planted in and around the avenue. Plaques adjacent to each tree give the names of those being honoured along with their country of residence during the war.

Marc Chagall windows in the Hadassah hospital

These are located in the Synagogue of the Hadassah Hebrew University, which is the largest medical centre in the Middle East. Chagall's stained-

Above: Yad Vashem is the Holocaust Museum in the New City of Jerusalem. It is designed to represent light at the end of a tunnel

glass windows depict the blessings that the patriarch Jacob bestowed on his twelve sons before he died (Genesis 49:1–27). The sons of Jacob became the founders of the twelve tribes of Israel.

Mea She'arim—The ultra-orthodox Jews

There is a district in the northwest of Jerusalem, called Mea She'arim. The name means 'hundredfold' and it is said to come from Genesis 26:12, 'Then Isaac sowed in that land, and reaped in the same year a hundredfold; and the LORD blessed him.' It was one of the earliest settlements outside the Old City, and originally it was surrounded by a wall with one hundred gates to protect the occupants from Arab raiders. Since 1887 it has become the home of ultra-orthodox Jews. It is a centre for Hassidic Jews, the descendants of Eastern European immigrants. The men are instantly recognisable in their black gowns and beaver-fur hats or wide-brimmed black felt hats. The boys wear short trousers with long black socks. Long curly side locks fall from beneath the hats of both the men and boys. The women dress with great modesty, wearing long dresses and keeping their arms, their shoulders and their heads covered.

In Mea She'arim, many of the buildings are either a synagogue, a theological institution (Yeshivot) or study school (Midrashim). Behind closed doors, scribes take great pains to accurately copy the Scriptures by hand. If you visit the cobbled streets of Mea She'arim on Shabbat (the Sabbath), do not drive your car as it is likely to be stoned!

Above: Dormition Abbey is a popular landmark on Mount Zion

Israelite Tower

It is believed that this marks the area where the Babylonians under King Nebuchadnezzar breached the wall surrounding ancient Jerusalem in 596 BC in the time of Jehoiakim. As a result of this the prophet Ezekiel was carried off into exile.

The Protestant cemetery

This is located on the hill near Zion gate in a quiet corner on Mount Zion. It was established by Presbyterian missionaries and it is the resting place of American and British missionary pioneers of the Ottoman period. Among those buried here is Oskar Schindler, the German businessman who managed to save the Jewish workers in his factory from certain death at the hands of the Nazis, and whose deeds became well-known through Steven Spielberg's film, *Schindler's List*. The writer of the hymn 'It is well with my soul,' Horatio G. Spafford, is also buried here, as is William Flinders Petrie, credited as the father of modern archaeology, whose gravestone faces the rising sun, and also the archaeologist James Leslie Starkey.

The Upper Room

The Room of the Last Supper lies just outside the Dormition Abbey behind the Franciscan house on Mount Zion. The Upper Room is a large hall with the ceiling supported by three columns which divides the room into three naves. This structure was built by the Crusaders in the early 14th century on top of a much older structure which, according to archaeological research, was a church-synagogue of the early Christian community of Jerusalem; however, it is unlikely to be the site of the Last Supper or of the coming of the Holy Spirit at Pentecost.

Skull Hill or Gordon's Calvary

A certain location for the cross of Jesus is at present impossible. However, there appears to be strong circumstantial evidence for thinking that Skull Hill, first

Above: *A wall plaque at Yad Vashem graphically recalls the Holocaust*

identified by General Charles Gordon when visiting Jerusalem in 1884, is the correct location. Close by, Gordon also identified an ancient tomb and he quite reasonably linked the two. The slope of Skull Hill has eroded badly in the last hundred years, but it is possible to see the eye sockets and the nose bridge that give it its name. Regardless, it must be noted that while the Bible locates the crucifixion as 'the place of a skull' (Matthew 27:33) it never claims that it was on a hill or that this place bore the resemblance of a skull. We cannot be sure what this hill looked like 2000 years ago.

The Roman custom was always to execute criminals outside the city gates on a well travelled road; this public spectacle was meant to serve as a clear warning to all who might rebel against the empire. At Passover each year an enormous number of people would have

The Palestinians

The Greek word Palestine first occurs in the work of the Ionian historian Herodotus writing in the 5th century BC. Herodotus is sometimes referred to as the 'Father of history' and he was contemporaneous with Queen Esther. He refers to a group distinct from the Phoenicians, who were in all probability the Philistines—from which the word Palestine is derived.

The British Mandate of Palestine included present day Jordan and the Palestinian territories of the West Bank and Gaza strip. At present the Palestinian territories comprise just the West Bank and Gaza strip. Following the establishment of Israel in 1948 as the national home of the Jewish people, the use of the terms 'Palestine' and 'Palestinian' in reference to Palestinian Jews has largely dropped from use. However the Palestinian national charter, as amended by the Palestinian Liberation Organisation in July 1948 defined 'Palestinians' as those Arab nationals who, until 1947, normally resided in Palestine regardless of whether they were evicted from it or stayed there. Christian believers amongst the Palestinians tend to be in communion with the Church of England.

Above: Gordon's Calvary is called Skull Hill because of its appearance. General Gordon believed that this was the Place of a Skull referred to in the Bible in John chapter 19

been in the vicinity of Jerusalem, and it appears that the north of the city was reserved for the Samaritans. As they remained at home and celebrated this feast on Mount Gerizim, this area would have been vacant at that crowded season, therefore allowing executions to take place. Some scholars also think that this is the location for the stoning of Stephen.

The Garden Tomb

The image of the Garden Tomb is world famous, and is believed by many to be the location of the tomb of Joseph of Arimathea, and therefore a possible site of the burial and resurrection of Jesus. The New Testament reveals that whilst the early Christians met in the Temple, there was no hint of them seeking to identify special places in connection with the life and work of Jesus. They

were making history and not writing a travelogue, so instead of proclaiming the location of a redundant tomb, they spoke of a risen Lord.

Officially the Garden Tomb Association maintains this only as a possible site for Christ's burial, though many are convinced of its authenticity. Those who believe it may be the site of the resurrection of Jesus Christ point to a number of features including: the proximity of Skull Hill, the Great Cistern that was used to store water for the garden, the wine press, indicating that it was a fruitful place, and the rock hewn tomb. They also maintain that there are marks of Christian veneration at the tomb which also prove its sanctity throughout the ages. Some archaeologists question the authenticity of this tomb because features suggest that it was originally constructed

Above: The Garden Tomb is thought by many to date from the 1st century, and early Christian symbols have been discovered on the walls inside

Above: 'He is not here: for he is risen'

in the time of the Old Testament and not a 'new tomb' as specifically stated in Scripture.

In the Garden is an 'Egyptian papyrus column capital' that may have come from an Egyptian building that lies under the nave of the nearby basilica of St Etienne. Could that building have been the tomb of Solomon's Egyptian Queen (2 Chronicles 8:11)?

Various famous preachers have spoken at services in the Garden Tomb grounds, including in 1905 General William Booth, founder of the Salvation Army. He also raised the Salvation Army flag here, and this flag was later draped over his coffin at his funeral in London. Rev. Bill White, a former Chaplain of the Garden Tomb, recalled how, 'Once I was standing by the entrance to the gardens, when a young tourist rushed into the grounds. He hurriedly took innumerable photographs and pausing for breath on the way out said to me, 'So, what's special about this place then?' White replied, 'Young man you are in such a hurry I will tell you in two words': pointing to the tomb he said, 'It's empty!'

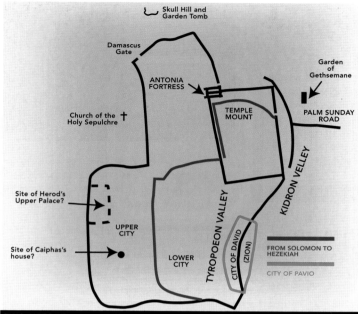

Skull Hill and
Garden Tomb

Damascus
Gate

Garden
of
Gethsemane

ANTONIA
FORTRESS

TEMPLE
MOUNT

PALM SUNDAY
ROAD

Church of the
Holy Sepulchre

KIDRON VALLEY

Site of Herod's
Upper Palace?

TYROPOEON VALLEY

CITY OF DAVID (ZION)

UPPER
CITY

FROM SOLOMON TO
HEZEKIAH

Site of Caiphas's
house?

LOWER
CITY

CITY OF PAVIO

TWO SITES FOR GOLGOTHA

TRAVEL INFORMATION

Unless otherwise noted
most places in this travel
section will be found
on the websites: www.
science.co.il/nature.
asp OR www.sacred-
destinations.com

Garden Tomb

Website: www.
gardentomb.com
The Garden Tomb is
one of the few sites
undeveloped. It is a
quiet place preserved for
worship and reflection.
There are places to sit
and drinking water is
available. There are
toilet facilities here, and
wheelchair access is good

Above: *Jeremiah's Grotto is next to the Garden Tomb*

for a general tour of
the Garden.

Directions: from the
Damascus Gate of the
Old City, cross the main
street and walk straight
up Nablus Road. The
Garden Tomb is located
on Conrad Schick Street,

a narrow lane on the right
hand side of Nablus Road.
It is clearly signposted.
Open six days a week,
but groups must book
in advance.

With prior arrangement,
facilities for celebrating
communion are available

to tour groups. There is also a well-stocked gift shop with very reasonable prices.

The Garden is owned and administered by The Garden Tomb (Jerusalem) Association, an evangelical charitable trust based in the United Kingdom.

Skull Hill

Is located behind the bus station on Sultan Suleiman, but can best be seen from the Garden Tomb platform. To the right of Skull Hill is the depression known as Jeremiah's Grotto, where the prophet is said to have lamented over Jerusalem.

Yad Vashem

The Holocaust Martyrs' and Heroes' Remembrance Authority P.O.Box 3477, Jerusalem 91034
Tel: (972) 2 6443400
Fax: (972) 2 6443443
Website: www. yadvashem.org
Opening hours: Sunday-Thursday 1000–1700
Friday and Eve of Jewish Holidays 0900–1400
Closed on Saturday and all Jewish Holidays.
Bus Routes: 13, 17, 17a, 18, 20, 21, 23, 24, 26, 27, 39, 99.

Above: *At Yad Vashem the Avenue of the Righteous among the Nations is a road with gardens bearing the names of those who risked or lost their lives to save Jews during the Holocaust*

OTHER PLACES OF INTEREST

Bible Lands Museum, Jerusalem

Museum Row, 25 Granot Street,
P.O Box 4670,
Jerusalem 91046
Website: www.blmj.org
☎ 972–2–5611066
It is the only museum in the world displaying the history of the biblical period in the various lands of the Bible.

The Israel Museum

Located on Ruppin Boulevard, near the Knesset (Israeli Parliament)
Website: http://www.imjnet.org.il/
☎ 972–2–670–8811
Here are many fascinating exhibits including the Dead Sea Scrolls which are housed in the Shrine of the Book and the Model of the Second Temple (see below).

Open: Sun, Mon, Wed, Thurs 1000–1700. Tues 1600–2100. Fri and holiday eves 1000–1400. Sat and holidays 1000–1700

The Shrine of the Book

Website: www.imj.org.il
This building houses the Dead Sea Scrolls. It is designed to resemble the lid of one of the jars in which the scrolls were found. Jets of water spray onto the building continually to maintain a constant temperature.

Open: As the Israel Museum (above).

The Model of Second Temple

Website: www.imj.org.il
This is a 1:50 model of Jerusalem at the time of the Second Temple.

Left: Talithakumi is just off Ben Yehuda Street and recalls Jesus healing the little girl

It provides a helpful overview of the city and the temple as it was at the time of Christ.
Open: As the Israel Museum (above).

The Rockefeller Museum

Sultan Suleiman Street East Jerusalem (Near the Flower gate)
This Museum is one of the largest and most impressive archaeological museums in Israel. It houses the collection of antiquities unearthed in the country mainly during the time of the British Mandate (1919–1948), and also a fragment of Mark 6 that was found in a cave in the Dead Sea area predating AD 70.

The Tower of David Museum—Jerusalem

Website: www.towerofdavid.org.il
Set in the magnificently restored ancient Citadel first constructed 2,000 years ago by Herod the Great, the Tower of David Museum traces Jerusalem's long and eventful history through state-of-the-art displays and exhibits. The panoramic route along the Citadel towers offers excellent views of the city.

Ben Yehuda Street

This street is named after Eliezer Ben Yehuda, who in the late 19th century almost single-handedly revived Hebrew as a modern spoken language. It is the heart of the downtown triangle formed with King George Street and Jaffa Road. If time permits this is a good place to relax and have refreshments.

Above: Ben Yehuda Street is a great place to meet friends for coffee

Timeline from Abraham to Solomon

This timeline assumes the accuracy of the ages and periods stated in the Old Testament.

BC	Event
2166	Abraham was born.
2091	Abraham left Haran at the age of 75 (Genesis 12:4).
2066	Isaac was born when Abraham was 100 (Genesis 21:5).
2006	Jacob was born when Isaac was 60 (Genesis 25:26).
1915	Joseph was born 17 years before entering Egypt which was 39 years before Jacob entered Egypt (Genesis 45:6 i.e. Joseph's age of 30 plus 7 years of plenty and 2 years of famine).
1898	Joseph was sold into Egyptian slavery at the age of 17 (Genesis 37:2).
1885	Joseph entered Pharaoh's service at the age of 30 (Genesis 41:46).
1876	Jacob settled in Egypt at the age of 130 (Genesis 47:9) and 430 years before the Exodus (Exodus 12:41).
1859	Jacob died at the age of 147 and 17 years after he settled in Egypt (Genesis 47:28).
1805	Joseph died at the age of 110 (Genesis 50:25).
1526	Birth of Moses—he was around 80 at the time of the Exodus (Exodus 7:7 and Acts 7:30).
1446	The Exodus: the Hebrews left Egypt 480 years before Solomon's fourth year (1 Kings 6:1). This guide assumes a 15th century date.
1406	Death of Moses at the age of 120, and the beginning of the conquest of Canaan (Deuteronomy 34:7).
	Joshua took command in his early 60s (on the basis that the 'young man' of Exodus 33:11 would not be much more than 20; see Numbers 14:26–30).
1399	Major battles for the Promised Land completed according to Caleb in Joshua 14:10.
1356	Joshua died at the age of 110 (Joshua 24:29).
1356–1050	Period of the Judges.
1050–1010	Saul's reign. Precise accuracy of these dates is not possible since Saul's exact age and length of reign in 1 Samuel 13:1 are not given.
1010–971	David's reign. He began at the age of 30 (2 Samuel 5:4) and therefore was born in 1040.
970–930	Solomon's reign (2 Chronicles 9:30).
966	This year is accepted by scholars as the fourth year of Solomon's reign. In this year he began to build the temple. This was 480 years after the Exodus (1 Kings 6:1). The Exodus itself was 430 years after Jacob settled in Egypt (Exodus 12:41).

Hebrew kings: The kingdom divided—Israel and Judah

The dates for Hebrew kings can be established accurately by connecting them with kings and events of surrounding nations (especially Egypt, Assyria, Babylonia and the Hittites) whose dates are sometimes given by astronomical data. As a result of this, for example, we can fix the year of Ahab's death as 853 BC, and this enables us to work both backwards and forwards from there using biblical data. Some are co–regencies.

Judah (20 kings reigning in Jerusalem)		Israel (20 kings reigning in Samaria)	
Rehoboam	930–913	Jeroboam I	930–909
Abijam	913–910	Nadab	909–908
Asa	910–869	Baasha	908–886
		Elah	886–884
		Zimri	885–884
		Tibni	885–880
		Omri	885–874
Jehoshaphat	870–848	Ahab	874–853
Jehoram	848–841	Ahaziah	853–852
Ahaziah	841	Joram	852–841
Athaliah	841–835	Jehu	841–814
Joash	835–796	Jehoahaz	814–798
Amaziah	796–767	Jehoash	798–82
Azariah	767–739	Jeroboam II	782–753
		Zachariah	753–752
		Shallum	752
		Menahem	752–742
Jotham	739–732	Pekahiah	742–739
		Pekah	737–732
Ahaz	732–716	Hoshea	732–723 fall of Samaria to Assyria (722).
Hezekiah	716–687 Sennacherib attacked Jerusalem in 701.		
Manasseh	687–642		
Amon	642–640		
Josiah	640–609		
Jehoahaz	609		
Jehoiakim	609–597 many Jews exiled to Babylon including Daniel and Ezekiel.		
	597		
	597–587 fall of Jerusalem to Babylon (16 March 597). More Jews into exile.		
	Final destruction in 587.		
	539 the fall of Babylon to Persia and Cyrus of Persia allows Jews to return and rebuild Jerusalem.		

118

Timeline of the main battles for Jerusalem

1010 BC?	David conquered Jerusalem and made it his capital.
701	Sennacherib, King of Assyria, unsuccessfully laid siege to Jerusalem.
586	Kingdom of Judah fell to Nebuchadnezzar, King of Babylon, who captured and destroyed Jerusalem, including the First Temple, and exiled Jews to Babylon.
350	Persians captured Jerusalem.
170	Antiochus Epiphanies, King of Syria, plundered Jerusalem.
165	25 Kislev (the third month of the civil year and the ninth month of the ecclesiastical year on the Jewish calendar). Jerusalem recaptured and Temple rededicated (celebrated at Hanukkah to this day).
63 BC	Roman invasion led by the Roman General Pompei.
AD 70	Siege of Jerusalem for 134 days by Romans under Vespasian, Jerusalem fell and the Second Temple was destroyed by Titus.
132–5	Second Jewish Revolt, led by Bar Kochba. Large scale slaughter, Jerusalem razed and then rebuilt by Hadrian and renamed 'Aelia Capitolina'. Jews excluded from Jerusalem.
614	Jerusalem fell to Persians.
629	Jerusalem retaken by Byzantines.
638	Caliph Omar Ben Hatav captured Jerusalem placing it under Arab rule.
1077	Turks captured Jerusalem.
1099	First Crusades re-captured Jerusalem. Many Jews and Muslims slaughtered. Godfrey of Bouillon led the attack and was named 'Protector of the Holy Sepulchre'.
1187	Saladin captured Jerusalem from Crusaders. Jewish settlement renewed.
1192	Richard the Lionheart failed to conquer Jerusalem.
1244	Jerusalem sacked by Tartars.
1259	Jerusalem sacked by Mongols. Jerusalem again conquered by Mamelukes.
1516–17	Turkish Sultan Selim conquered Jerusalem for the Ottoman Empire.
1535	Jerusalem conquered by Mehemet Ali of Egypt.
1917	British Army entered Jerusalem under General Allenby.
1918–20	Jerusalem under British military administration.
1948	February: TransJordanian army shelled Jewish Quarter. 14th May: British Mandate ended. 15th May: State of Israel proclaimed. 19th May: Arab siege of the Old City lifted. 28th May: Jewish Quarter of the Old City fell to Jordanian Legionnaires. 26th July: Western Jerusalem proclaimed Israeli territory.
1967	5 to 11 June: Six Day War. 7th June: Old City captured by Israel.

Timeline of Roman emperors and Jewish rulers

Roman Emperors

27 BC–AD14 Augustus. Birth of Jesus Christ

14–37 Tiberius. Life and death of Jesus Christ. He recalls Pilate to Rome.

37–41 Gaius (Caligula). The conversion of Paul and the formation of the church.

41–54 Claudius. Acts 11:28 and 18:2.

54–68 Nero. Persecution of Christians, martyrdom of Peter and Paul. Some of his household converted (Philippians 4:22).

68–69 Galba, Otho. Each soon assassinated or killed in battle. Vitellius.

69–79 Vespasian. Ordered the destruction of Jerusalem in AD 70.

79–81 Titus. Destroyed Jerusalem in AD 70 as commander of the army.

81–96 Domitian. Possibly in his reign John was exiled on Patmos.

Jewish Rulers

37–4 BC Herod the Great. Birth of Jesus, ordered death of boys in Bethlehem.

4 BC–AD 6 Herod Archelaus. Joseph, Mary and Jesus return from exile in Egypt.

4 BC–AD 39 Herod Antipas. Ordered the death of John the Baptist.

4 BC–AD 34 Philip Herodias. His wife married Antipas.

AD 37–44 Herod Agrippa I. Beheaded James the brother of John.

AD 44–93 Herod Agrippa II. Had oversight of the Temple and listened to Paul at Caesarea.

Timeline of The Holy Land

Second Temple Period:

37 BC to AD 70 King Herod built the Jerusalem Temple during this time. To be precise it was the third Temple, because the second Temple was built when the Jews returned from Babylon around 587 BC.

Judeo/Christian Period:

The time between the resurrection of Jesus Christ and the establishment of the first purpose-built churches in the 3rd century by Constantine.

Constantine Period:

The Roman Emperor Constantine (AD 274–337) converted to Christianity through the influence of his mother Helena. He then ordered the building of churches in the Holy Land.

Byzantine Period:

This is the period of seven centuries between the death of Constantine and the arrival of the Crusaders in the 11th century.

Crusader Period:

AD 1096–1187. During a relatively brief period of less than a century, the Crusaders built many churches, often on the ruins of Byzantine churches. They were defeated by Saladin at the Horns of Hattin in AD 1187 but kept coastal control of Acre until AD 1291.

Middle Ages:

Islam became the dominant force in Palestine after the defeat of the Crusaders. However, their acceptance of Jesus Christ as a prophet meant that some churches were still occupied during this period by monastic communities, mainly Augustinian, Benedictine and Franciscan.

Modern Times:

Since 1900, increased missionary activity has led to the building of new churches all across Israel.

INFORMATION FOR THE TRAVELLER IN ISRAEL

Medical

Israel does not require any special inoculations and it has well stocked pharmacies. Good sunscreen cream is advisable as the sun is very strong in Israel. Sunglasses are essential.

Documents

Photocopy your passport (and keep the copy with you at all times), travel insurance, repeat prescription form, and glasses specification. Leave a copy of these, and an itinerary and address of your travel company, with your home contact person—either as a scanned email attachment or a hard copy.

Footwear and clothing

Comfortable shoes are essential for the day, and a change for the evening.

Loose cotton clothing will help you to stay cool. Due to the political sensitivities avoid wearing any shirts that refer to a western country. A hat is a must for the heat of the day. Swimwear is always useful as there are many places for swimming.

When visiting religious sites, like churches and mosques, ladies must avoid shorts and bare arms and shoulders. Men must avoid shorts and will have to wear shirts with sleeves to gain access to these sites. If these sites are mixed in with other locations on a particular day, then ladies could put into their hand luggage a lightweight shawl and wrap around skirt. Men could pack lightweight tracksuit trousers that can be slipped over shorts, and something over a short sleeved shirt.

The evenings are much cooler, so include a light-weight jumper or cardigan. Don't forget lightweight waterproofs and a torch if you plan to walk Hezekiah's Tunnel or other underground sites.

Drinks and water

Apart from hotels or reputable restaurants, avoid freshly squeezed fruit juice at tourist sites. Mineral water is readily available and is preferable to tap water. It would be best to clean teeth with mineral water as well.

Photography

Care must be taken when photographing modern sites (police, airports, bridges etc.). It is unwise to photograph people without their permission and especially women—particularly if they are veiled.

Luggage and labelling

Label all your luggage with only your name, tour operator and first hotel. For home, use only a house number and post code. Put full details with a list of where you will be staying inside the locked case.

Follow carefully the airline instructions for what not to carry in your hand luggage. Ladies do pack a spare bra in your hand luggage, as this item may prove difficult to replace in the size you are comfortable with.

You will want to carry with you each day: water, hat, sun cream, camera, tissues etc, so pack a bag for this.

Money

The travel company can advise on the amount. It is best to use travellers cheques and to keep a copy of their numbers. A credit card is useful for back up, but be careful of interest charges. On arrival in Israel, money changing should be arranged by the tour operator. If travelling alone use a reputable outlet, like a bank or hotel. Small denomination American dollars are useful for tips and emergencies. Ensure wallets and purses are secure at all times.

RECOMMENDED READING

Through the British Museum with the Bible by Brian Edwards and Clive Anderson, published by Day One.
ISBN 978 1 84625 124 5.
Discoveries from Bible Times by Alan Millard published by Lion
ISBN 978 0 7459 3740 3.

AUTHORS

Paul Williams is the Pastor of Swindon Evangelical Church. He also serves on the board of the European Missionary Fellowship (EMF), and lectures in systematic theology at their School of Biblical Studies. He enjoys leading tours to Israel and he is also the author of *Travel with William Cowper* in this series. Paul is married to Ruth, and they have three children.

Clive Anderson is the Pastor of the Butts Church in Alton, Hants. He is a member of The British Museum Society, The British Institute for the Study of Iraq, the Egypt Exploration Society and the Tyndale Society; he leads tours to the Middle East and around the British Museum and is the author of eight books including *Travel with Spurgeon* in this series. Clive is married to Amanda, and they have one son.

ACKNOWLEDGEMENTS

Mark and Lynne Trafford, together with Duncan and Andrea Thew, for some of the photographs used.

This series is unique: each book combines biography and history with travel guide. Notes, maps and photographs help you to explore Britain's distinctive heritage.

Oxford: City of saints, scholars and dreaming spires
Cambridge: City of beauty, reformation and pioneering research

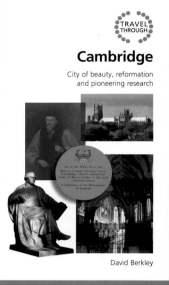

128 pages   £10 EACH

- **PLACES OF INTEREST**
- **PACKED WITH COLOUR PHOTOS**
- **CLEAR ILLUSTRATED MAPS**
- **GREAT GIFT IDEA**

THROUGH THE BRITISH MUSEUM
ISBN 978 1 903087 54 1
TRAVEL WITH JOHN BUNYAN
ISBN 978 1 903087 12 1
TRAVEL WITH C H SPURGEON
ISBN 978 1 903087 11 4
TRAVEL WITH WILLIAM BOOTH
ISBN 978 1 903087 35 X
TRAVEL WITH JOHN KNOX
ISBN 978 1 903087 35 0
TRAVEL WITH MARTYN LLOYD-JONES
ISBN 978 1 903087 58 9
TRAVEL WITH WILLIAM GRIMSHAW
ISBN 978 1 903087 68 8
TRAVEL WITH WILLIAM CAREY
ISBN 978 1 903087 76 3
TRAVEL WITH WILLIAM WILBERFORCE
ISBN 978 1 84625 027 9
TRAVEL WITH C S LEWIS
ISBN 978 1 84625 056 9

TRAVEL WITH ROBERT MURRAY McCHEYNE
ISBN 978 1 84625 057 6
MARTYRS OF MARY TUDOR
ISBN 978 1 842625 0033
TRAVEL THROUGH OXFORD
ISBN X978 1 84625 115 3
TRAVEL THROUGH CAMBRIDGE
ISBN 978 1 84625 119 1

A series of children's activity books twinned with selected Travel Guides

WILLIAM BOOTH
ISBN 1 903087 83 X

JOHN BUNYAN
ISBN 1 903087 81 3

WILLIAM CAREY
ISBN 1 846250 12 9

WILLIAM WILBERFORCE
ISBN 1 84625 028 5

C S LEWIS
ISBN 1 84625 056 9

KINGS, PHARAOHS AND BANDITS—THE OLD TESTAMENT IN THE BRITISH MUSEUM
ISBN 978 1 84625 035 4

ROMANS, GLADIATORS AND GAMES—THE NEW TESTAMENT IN THE BRITISH MUSEUM
ISBN 978 1 84625 036 1

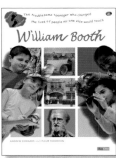

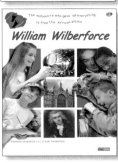

Permission is given to copy the activity pages and associated text for use as class or group material

YOUR NOTES

YOUR NOTES

YOUR NOTES